THE HEINEMANN
ACCOUNTANCY AND ADMINISTRATION SERIES

General Editor: J. BATTY
D.COM.(S.A.), M.COM.(DUNELM), A.C.W.A., M.I.O.M., M.B.I.M.

AN OUTLINE OF THE
LAW OF TRUSTS

AN OUTLINE OF THE
LAW OF TRUSTS

A. F. CHICK, F.C.A.

HEINEMANN:LONDON

William Heinemann Ltd

LONDON MELBOURNE TORONTO

CAPE TOWN AUCKLAND

© A. F. Chick 1968
First published 1968
434 90230 6

Made in Great Britain at the Pitman Press, Bath

Editor's Foreword

THE Heinemann Accountancy and Administration Series is intended to fill a gap in the literature that caters for accountants, company secretaries, and similar professional people who are engaged in giving a vital information service to management.

This book, *An Outline of the Law of Trusts*, presents an important but difficult subject in a concise and readable manner. The author has made a study of the subject over many years and his *Apportionment in relation to Trust Accounts* has long been accepted as an authoritative textbook and work of reference.

Intended primarily for students following the syllabus of the Institute of Chartered Accountants in England and Wales, it may possibly meet the requirements of other professional bodies requiring an outline knowledge of the subject.

The book is a welcome addition to the series. I hope that to students, practitioners, and staffs of trust corporations it will prove of great assistance. My belief is that this hope will be amply fulfilled.

Aberdeen   J. BATTY

Preface

THIS short work has been written primarily to meet the requirements of candidates preparing for the Final examination of the Institute of Chartered Accountants in England and Wales.

Why do professional accountants require a knowledge of trusts? Firstly, because few are fortunate enough to escape the onerous duties of trusteeship, and the standard of care required from professional trustees is usually higher than that expected of laymen. Secondly, to enable them to carry out the audit of trust accounts expertly. With this in mind, the Trustee Investments Act, 1961, has been reproduced in full in Appendix B. Thirdly, because the complexities of taxation today make a knowledge of trusts essential if efficient service is to be rendered to clients.

If the *Outline* was to be kept within reasonable bounds, some omissions were inevitable. Amongst these are Settled Land and Mutual Wills.

A great debt of gratitude is due to Mr G. R. E. Wallis, LL.B., Solicitor, who read the manuscript and made many valuable suggestions. But any errors or omissions are mine and mine alone. Acknowledgment must also be made to the Incorporated Council of Law Reporting for England and Wales for its kind permission to reproduce extracts from judgments from reports, the copyright of which is vested in the Council.

A.F.C.

Contents

Page

CHAPTER 9 MISCELLANEOUS MATTERS

CONTENTS

Table of Cases

Table of Statutes

Page

Statutory Instruments

List of Works Cited

Lewin on Trusts, 16th edition, 1964 (Sweet & Maxwell Ltd.)

Maitland's Equity, 2nd edition, 1936 (Cambridge University Press)

Nathan's Equity through the Cases, 4th edition, 1961 (Stevens & Sons Ltd.)
[Fifth edition under the title: Nathan & Marshall. *A Casebook on Trusts*. 1968]

Underhill's Law of Trusts and Trustees, 11th edition, 1959, with 1966 Supplement (Butterworth & Company Ltd.)

Addenda

The following should be noted as arising from the Finance Act, 1968:

Page 14   *Gifts in consideration of marriage. See* section 36, Finance Act, 1868, as regards the restrictions on the exemption of such gifts from estate duty, in case of a gift made after 19 March 1968 and in the case of a death after that date.

Page 15   *Discretionary trusts and estate duty. See* section 39, Finance Act, 1968, as to the charge to estate duty in the case of a death after 19 March 1968 if a discretionary trust is limited on a death.

Page 61   *Gifts made within five years of death.* Section 35, Finance Act, 1968, substitutes seven years for five years in the case of a death after 19 March 1968, except as respects a period beginning on or before 19 March 1963.

1 Introduction

(A) WHAT IS A TRUST?

MAITLAND stated that of all the exploits of Equity the largest and the most important is the invention and development of the Trust[1] but confessed it was difficult to find an authoritative definition. Sir Arthur Underhill, in his *Law of Trusts and Trustees*[2] gave the following definition:

'A trust is an equitable obligation, binding a person (who is called a trustee) to deal with property over which he has control (which is called the trust property) for the benefit of persons (who are called the beneficiaries or *cestuis que trust*) of whom he may himself be one, and any one of whom may enforce the obligation. Any act or neglect on the part of a trustee which is not authorised or excused by the terms of the trust instrument, or by law, is called a breach of trust.'[3]

Although this definition may be criticised in that it does not cover charitable trusts[4] or trusts of imperfect obligation,[5] it does for our present purpose bring out the essentials of the subject.

(B) CONTRAST WITH OTHER LEGAL RELATIONSHIPS

(1) TRUSTS AND CONTRACTS

A beneficiary of a completely constituted trust,[6] though not as such a party to the document creating the trust, can as stated above enforce the obligation. With certain exceptions, a person who is not a party to a contract cannot sue upon it even if it purports to be made for his benefit.[7] This rule was stated by Lord Haldane in *Dunlop Pneumatic Tyre Co.* v. *Selfridge*:[8]

'My Lords, in the law of England, certain principles are fundamental. One is that only a person who is a party to the contract can sue on it. Our law knows

---

[1] *Equity*, Lecture III.
[2] 11th ed., p. 3.
[3] Cited by Romer, L.J., in *Green* v. *Russell*, [1959] 2 Q.B. 226, 241.
[4] *See* Chapter 3, p. 16.
[5] *post*, p. 19.
[6] For the meaning of this expression, *see* Chapter 3, p. 12.
[7] *Per* Salmon, L.J., in *Beswick* v. *Beswick*, [1966] 3 W.L.R. 396, 412.
[8] [1915] A.C. 847, 853. Accepted by Lord Wright in *Vanderpitte* v. *Preferred Accident Corporation of New York*, [1933] A.C. 70, 79.

nothing of a *jus quaesitum tertio* arising by way of contract. Such a right may be conferred by way of property as, for example under a trust, but it cannot be conferred on a stranger to a contract as a right to enforce the contract *in personam*.'

An example is provided by *In re Miller's Agreement*.[9] There two partners covenanted with a retiring partner that on his death they would pay certain annuities to his daughters, but no trust was created in their favour. The daughters, not being parties to the agreement, had no right to sue for their annuities, with the consequence that the Revenue could not found a claim to estate duty under section 2(1)(*d*), Finance Act, 1894, on the basis that a beneficial interest had been provided by the father for his daughters.

Among the exceptions may be noted:

(*a*) If by reason of the construction of the contract, or the special circumstances in which the contract is entered into, the true effect of the contract is that one of the contracting parties is contracting as trustee for the third party.[10] But it is not legitimate to import into the contract the idea of a trust when the parties have given no indication that such was their intention.[11]

For example, in *In re Foster's Policy*[12] a testator took out a policy in 1931 'on the life of and for the benefit of' his daughter. The policy provided that in the event of the daughter's death before 'the option anniversary', 2 February 1954, the premiums would be returned to the testator or his estate, and up to and including that date the testator or his personal representative had the right (without the consent of the daughter) to surrender, to reduce or to borrow on the policy. After the option anniversary these rights were vested in and for the benefit of the daughter, her personal representatives or assigns. The father paid the premiums until his death on 2 September 1939, and thereafter they were paid by his personal representatives. On the option anniversary they exercised the option to convert the policy into a policy for the benefit of the daughter and on 29 July 1955, the personal representatives at the request of the daughter assigned the policy to her and thereafter the annual premiums were paid by the daughter.

Plowman, J., held that since a time came when according to the terms of the policy, the testator ceased to be entitled to any beneficial interest under it, namely the date of the option anniversary and from that date the right to

[9] [1947] Ch. 615. Although this decision of Wynn-Parry, J., was doubted by Lord Denning, M.R., in the Court of Appeal in *Beswick* v. *Beswick*, [1966] 3 W.L.R. 396, when that case went to the House of Lords, Lord Reid said the decision was clearly right, [1967] 3 W.L.R. at p. 938 (E).
[10] *Per* Tomlin, J., in *Royal Exchange Assurance* v. *Hope*, [1928] Ch. 179.
[11] *Per* Lord Greene, M.R., in *In re Schebsman*, [1944] Ch. 83, 89.
[12] [1966] 1 W.L.R. 222.

surrender the policy or to reduce or to borrow upon it became vested in the daughter for her own benefit, the policy gave rise to a trust of the assurance moneys for the benefit of the daughter.[13]

(b) A policy of assurance effected by a man on his own life, and expressed to be for the benefit of his wife, or of his children, or of his wife and children, or any of them, creates a trust in favour of the objects named therein.[14]

(c) The Court will, in certain circumstances, decree specific performance of a contract between A and B expressed to be for the benefit of C. In *Beswick* v. *Beswick*[15] by an agreement in writing P.B. agreed with his nephew that he would transfer to the nephew the goodwill and trade utensils of his business in consideration of the nephew undertaking first to pay him £6 10s. 0d. per week for the remainder of his life and then to pay to P.B.'s widow an annuity of £5 per week in the event of her husband's death. On P.B.'s death the nephew made one payment of £5 but refused to make any further payment to her. Although the widow in her personal capacity could not enforce the agreement, yet in her capacity of administratrix of her husband's estate she could enforce the provision of the agreement for the benefit of herself in her personal capacity, and the proper way of enforcing that provision is to order specific performance.[16] Lord Pearce in giving his opinion in this case said[17] that the defendant on his side had received the whole benefit of the contract and it was a matter of conscience for the Court to see that he now performed his part of it, and quoted Kay, J., in *Hart* v. *Hart:*[18]

'. . . when an agreement for valuable consideration has been partially performed, the court ought to do its utmost to carry out that agreement by a decree for specific performance.'

(2) TRUSTS AND BAILMENTS

Take the case of A, the owner of a valuable painting, delivering the painting to B for the purpose of having it cleaned. A is the bailor and B is the bailee. As such B is under an obligation to carry out the work and then to return the painting to A. If B, contrary to the terms of the bailment, sells the painting to C, then, in general, C would get no title to the goods, since B was not the owner and could not confer a good title on C.

Compare this with the case of A, on the occasion of his son's marriage,

---

[13] The assurance moneys could not, under the terms of the policy, become payable until after the option anniversary.
[14] Married Women's Property Act, 1882, s.11. The Policy in *In re Foster's Policy, supra,* was not written under this Act.
[15] [1967] 3 W.L.R. 932.
[16] *Per* Lord Reid at p. 940 (F).
[17] ibid., at p. 950 (C).
[18] (1881) 18 Ch. D. 670, 685.

making a settlement by vesting the ownership of property (including the valuable painting) in B as trustee for the benefit of his son and issue. B in breach of trust sells the painting to C who buys in good faith and without notice of the trust. C gets a good title, since B was the owner of the goods and could pass his title to C. The beneficiary under the settlement would have no rights against C.

(3) TRUSTEES AND PERSONAL REPRESENTATIVES

The distinction here is a matter of history,[19] but space will not permit this to be traced. Suffice it to say that:

(a) If A and B are personal representatives of a deceased's estate, either can sell and give the purchaser a good title to personalty. In other words, their authority is joint and several.

(b) In the case of realty the authority is joint. A sole personal representative can give a good title to real estate, but if there are two or more personal representatives all must join in to give a good title.

(c) A sole trustee can give a good title to personalty, but (except where a trust corporation is the trustee) he cannot sell realty. If there are two or more trustees, then all must concur, whether the property is personalty or realty. In other words the authority of trustees is joint for all classes of property.[20]

A personal representative is not a trustee for a legatee until he has assented to the bequest.[21]

In many cases it may be difficult to determine when personal representatives cease to be such and become trustees.

(C) THE NATURE OF AN EQUITABLE INTEREST

The trustee has control of the trust property, according to the definition given earlier in this chapter; the beneficiary can enforce the trust in his favour. If the trustee lets property held by him in trust and the tenant falls in arrear with the rent, can the beneficiary distrain for the rent? That was the question in *Schalit* v. *Joseph Nadler*[22] and Goddard, J., in delivering the judgment in that case explained the nature of a beneficiary's interest in these words:

'The right of the *cestui que trust* whose trustee has demised property subject to the trust is, not to the rent, but to an account from the trustee of the profits

[19] Maitland's *Equity*, p. 48.
[20] *Attenborough* v. *Solomon*, [1913] A.C. 76.
[21] ibid.
[22] [1933] 2 K.B. 79.

received from the demise. . . . The *cestui que trust* has no right to demand that the actual banknotes received by the trustee shall be handed over to him, or that a cheque for rent drawn to the trustee shall be endorsed over. What he can require is that the trustee shall account to him, after taking credit for any outgoings or other payments properly chargeable, for the profits received from the trust property.'

In the revenue case of *Baker* v. *Archer-Shee*[23] the point arose whether for purpose of assessment to income tax a beneficiary's income from an American trust arose from 'stocks, shares or rents' or from a foreign possession. Although for reasons connected with taxation law the House of Lords, by a majority, decided that the income arose from stocks and shares, Lord Sumner in his speech explained the general equity view in this way:

'The position of the equitable tenant for life and of the investments which form the trust fund is so clear, both in law and equity, that, apart from any special prescriptions, express or implied, of the law relating to income tax, there can, I think, be no doubt about them. The trustee has the full legal property[24] in the whole of the trust fund and the beneficiary has not. Apart from special provisions in particular settlements, which do not affect the general principle, the trustee is not the agent of the beneficiary, who can neither appoint nor dismiss him. She cannot require him to change or forbid him to change the particular investments of the fund. There is no liability on the beneficiary for the trustee's acts on the principle of *respondeat superior* and, unless the trust deed otherwise provides, he must act without remuneration to himself and cannot in any case sue the beneficiary on any implied promise to pay. It is the trustee alone who can give a discharge for interest, rent or dividends to the parties who have to pay them in respect of the invested trust estate, nor need they know the beneficiary in the matter. All that the latter can do is to claim the assistance of a court of equity to enforce the trust and to compel the trustee to discharge it. This right is quite as good and often is better than any legal right, but it is not in any case one which for all purposes makes the trust fund "belong" to the beneficiary or makes the income of it accrue to him *eo instanti* and directly as it leaves the hand of the party who pays it.'

Compare this with the long-established rule that until the administration of a deceased's estate is completed, the residue does not come into existence and accordingly the residuary legatee has no beneficial interest in the testator's assets or the income arising therefrom during administration. All he has is a chose in action.[25] The next-of-kin of an intestate are in a similar position.[26]

---

[23] [1927] A.C. 844.
[24] As will be explained in Chapter 3, the trust fund may consist of an equitable interest in property.
[25] *Sudely (Lord)* v. *Attorney-General*, [1897] A.C. 11; *Commissioners of Stamp Duties (Queensland)* v. *Livingston*, [1964] 3 W.L.R. 963.
[26] *Eastbourne Mutual Building Society* v. *Hastings Corporation*, [1965] 1 W.L.R. 861; *Lall* v. *Lall*, [1965] 1 W.L.R. 1249.

2 Classification of Trusts

FOR convenience it is desirable to classify trusts and in view of the wording of section 53 (1), Law of Property Act, 1925,[1] it is advisable to do so though the authorities are not wholly unanimous in the matter.

All trusts are either, first, express trusts which are raised and created by act of the parties, or implied trusts, which are raised or created by act or construction of law.[2]

If there is created in expressed terms, whether written or verbal (*quaere*, parol) a trust, and a person is in terms nominated[3] to be the trustee of the trust . . . such a trust is in equity called an express trust.[4]

(A) EXPRESS TRUSTS

Express trusts are divided into:

(1) Express private trusts
(2) Express public trusts (charitable trusts)

and include not only simple trusts, but also precatory trusts and discretionary trusts.

Precatory trusts, as where a testator devises an estate to A and his heirs 'not doubting' that he will thereout pay an annuity of £50 to B for his life, are, according to Lewin, express trusts, 'because in such cases the Court finds as a matter of construction that the settlor expressed directly an intention to create a trust'.[5]

A discretionary trust is one in which a number of objects[6] of the trust are designated and the trustees are given power to apply the income, and sometimes the capital, for the benefit of such of the beneficiaries as they in their absolute discretion think fit. Discretionary trusts are frequently linked with protective trusts where a beneficiary is given a life interest in a fund, determinable in the event of some act on his part, whereby the income

---

[1] *post*, p. 8.
[2] *Per* Nottingham, L.C., in *Cook* v. *Fountain* (1676) 3 Swanst. 585, 592.
[3] The trustee may have been appointed by the Court under section 41, Trustee Act, 1925.
[4] *Per* Lord Esher, M.R., in *Soar* v. *Ashwell*, [1893] 2 Q.B. 390, 393.
[5] *Lewin on Trusts*, 16th ed., p. 8.
[6] They may be charities or individuals.

may become payable to, for example, a trustee in bankruptcy. When such an act brings about a forfeiture, the trustees are directed to pay or apply the income to or for the benefit of a number of designated individuals (usually the life tenant, his wife and children) as the trustees in their absolute discretion think fit. Here we have an illustration of the rule that a trust is imperative, a mere power discretionary. The distinction will be discussed further in Chapter 3.

One further division of express trusts may be noticed, that between executed and executory trusts. An executed trust is one in which the intentions of the settlor have been completely stated, or as it is sometimes said, the settlor has been his own conveyancer, whilst an executory trust is one in which some further deed or instrument is necessary before the limitations of the beneficial interests are clearly defined.

Maitland put it this way:[7]

'The distinction becomes important in the construction of wills. A testator may either himself make a settlement or may sketch out a settlement that is to be made after his death. Well, the rule comes to this that in the latter case you will have a little more latitude in considering what the testator really meant than you will have in the former.'

For a fuller treatment of the distinction reference may be made to Keeton's *Law of Trusts*, 8th ed., p. 60.

(B) TRUSTS BY ACT OR CONSTRUCTION OF LAW, OR IMPLIED TRUSTS

This class includes:

(1) Resulting trusts
(2) Constructive trusts

A resulting trust occurs where property is settled or devised upon limitations that do not exhaust it, so that a resulting trust of the unexhausted part is left in the settlor or devisor.[8]

A constructive trust arises when the conduct and behaviour of a person in relation to property of which he is not an express trustee is such that the Court construes it as involving him in the duties and responsibilities of a trustee. As an example, a tenant for life of leaseholds renews the lease on his own account. In this case the law regards him as a constructive trustee, holding the renewed lease for those interested in the old lease.[9]

Further instances of resulting and constructive trusts will be given in Chapter 4.

---

[7] *Equity*, p. 63.
[8] *Per* Astbury, J., *In re Llanover Settled Estates*, [1926] Ch. 626, 637.
[9] *Keech* v. *Sandford* (1726) 2 Eq. Cas. Abr. 741; *Protheroe* v. Protheroe, [1968] 1 W.L.R. 519.

Law of Property Act, 1925, section 53, reads:

(1) Subject to the provisions hereinafter contained with respect to the creation of interests in land by parol . . .

  (b) a declaration of trust respecting any land or any interest therein must be manifested and proved by some writing signed by some person who is able to declare such trust or by his will; . . .

(2) This section does not affect the creation or operation of resulting, implied or constructive trusts.

3 Trusts Created by Act of Party

(A) EXPRESS PRIVATE TRUSTS

(1) PARTIES

(a) Settlor

In general any person entitled to the beneficial interest in any property and not subject to any legal restraint may create a trust. Such interest may extend to the legal estate or an equitable interest.

The capacity of certain persons requires consideration.

(i) *Infants*

An infant cannot hold a legal estate in land, so that a settlement by him of such a legal estate cannot be made. But a settlement of an equitable interest in land, or of personalty, can be made by an infant but is voidable on his part within a reasonable time of attaining his majority.

'A Court of Chancery has never claimed for itself a power to direct a settlement of an infant's property. Indeed it has more than once been stated authoritatively[1] that it cannot do so. . . .'[2] But under the Infants' Settlements Act, 1855, a male of not less than twenty and a female of not less than seventeen may, with the consent of the Court, make a binding settlement on his or her marriage.

(ii) *Married Women*

With the removal by statute in 1949 of the restraint on anticipation, it would appear that nowadays there are no impediments to a married woman making a settlement of her property.

(iii) *Corporations*

A trading company incorporated under the Companies Act, 1948, has an implied power to borrow money. Frequently it exercises this power by issuing debenture stock secured by a trust deed which it executes in favour of trustees on behalf of the debenture holders.

---

[1] *In re Leigh* (1888) 40 Ch.D.290.
[2] *Per* Wilberforce, J., in *In re T's Settlement Trusts*, [1963] 3 W.L.R.987, 990.

9

(b) Trustees

According to Lewin 'a trustee should be a person capable of taking and holding the legal estate, and possessed of natural capacity and legal ability to execute the trust, and domiciled within the jurisdiction of a Court of Equity'.[3]

(i) *Infants*

The appointment of an infant as a trustee of any settlement or trust is void.[4]

(ii) *Married Woman*

A married woman can be a trustee or personal representative in like manner as if she were a *femme sole*.[5]

(iii) *Bankrupts*

A bankrupt can be appointed a trustee.

(iv) *Beneficiaries*

Although it is undesirable that a *cestui que trust* should be a trustee, since there may be a conflict between his rights as a beneficiary and his duty as a trustee, there is no legal impediment to such an appointment.

(v) *Trust Corporations*

Nowadays many banks and insurance companies act as trustees and personal representatives. To enable them to do so they must be trust corporations as defined by the Law of Property Act, 1925,[6] and Rule 1 of the Public Trustee (Custodian Trustee) Rules, 1926, that is to say:

(1) the Public Trustee,
(2) a corporation appointed by the Court,
(3) a corporation entitled to act as custodian trustee.

A corporation so entitled is any corporation constituted under the law of the United Kingdom or any part thereof, having a place of business there, empowered by its constitution to undertake trust business, and being either

(a) a company incorporated by special Act or Royal Charter; or
(b) a company having an issued share capital for the time being of not

---

[3] *Lewin on Trusts*, 16th ed., p. 13.
[4] Law of Property Act, 1925, s.20.
[5] ibid., s.170.
[6] ibid., s.205 (1) (xxviii).

less than £250,000, of which not less than £100,000 has been paid up in cash; or

(c) an unlimited company, one of the members of which is a company within (a) or (b) above.

By the Law of Property (Amendment) Act, 1926, section 3, this definition is extended to include the Treasury Solicitor, the Official Solicitor and certain other officials, e.g. a trustee in bankruptcy, in relation to the property of the bankrupt.

Except where the trustee is a trust corporation, it is desirable to have two trustees, since a sole individual trustee cannot give a valid receipt for the proceeds of sale of land, or certain other capital moneys.[7] On the other hand, in the case of settlements and dispositions on trust for sale of land, the number of trustees must not exceed four. If more than four persons are named as trustees, the four first named (who are able and willing to act) will be the trustees, and the other persons named will not be trustees unless appointed on the occurrence of a vacancy. This limitation does not apply in the case of land vested in trustees for charitable, ecclesiastical, or public purposes.[8] Again when personal representatives appoint trustees of an infant's property, they must appoint a trust corporation, or two or more individuals not exceeding four.[9]

(c) Beneficiary

If an express private trust is to be upheld, there must be a beneficiary who can apply to the Court to compel the performance of the obligation in his favour.

(2) PROPERTY

The property subject to the trust may be the legal estate or an equitable interest in land or personalty.

(3) THE THREE CERTAINTIES

(a) Intention

For a trust to be upheld the Court must find a clear intention to impose an obligation and the language used must be definite enough to enable the

[7] Trustee Act, 1925, s.14 (2).
[8] ibid., s.34.
[9] Administration of Estates Act, 1925, s.42.

Court to ascertain what the precise obligation is. The intention may be expressly stated or, in the case of a precatory trust, may be inferred as a matter of construction of the document as a whole.[10]

(b) Subject matter

The property which is to be subject to the obligation imposed by the settlor must be certain. Here it may be said that a person within the jurisdiction may create a trust of foreign moveables, since under private international law moveables follow the person. But there appears to be considerable doubt whether a trust of foreign immoveables could be created.

(c) Object

That there must be certainty of object is another way of saying that there must be a beneficiary capable of being clearly identified by the Court as the person who can compel the performance of the trust in his favour.

(4) COMPLETELY AND INCOMPLETELY CONSTITUTED TRUSTS

Before explaining the distinction here, it will be in view that the creation of a trust may be a purely voluntary act on the part of the settlor, in which case the beneficiary is said to be a volunteer. If a person is not to be regarded as a volunteer, then either:

(a) he must have given valuable consideration for the promise by the proposed settlor to create a trust in his favour, or

(b) if the promise was to make a marriage settlement he must be within the marriage consideration.

If the settlor has done everything required of him to transfer the property to the trustees of the settlement, so that the trust is completely constituted then it matters not whether the beneficiary is a volunteer or not. The Court will assist him to compel performance of the trust.

If on the other hand the trust is not completely constituted, and the intended beneficiary is a volunteer the rule is: 'Equity will not assist a volunteer'.

The governing principle is set out in the judgment of Turner, L.J., in *Milroy* v. *Lord*:[11]

'I take the law of this Court to be well settled, that, in order to render a voluntary settlement valid and effectual, the settlor must have done everything which, according to the nature of the property comprised in the settlement, was

---

[10] *In re Williams*, [1897] 2 Ch. 12.
[11] (1862) 4 de G. F. & J. 264.

necessary to be done in order to transfer the property and render the settlement binding upon him. He may, of course, do this by actually transferring the property to the persons for whom he intends to provide, and the provision will then be effectual, and it will be equally effectual if he transfers the property to a trustee for the purposes of the settlement, or declares that he himself holds it in trust for those purposes; and if the property be personal, the trust may, as I apprehend, be declared either in writing or by parol; but, in order to render the settlement binding, one or other of these modes must, as I understand the law of this court, be resorted to, for there is no equity in this court to perfect an imperfect gift. The cases, I think, go further to this extent; that if the settlement is intended to be effectuated by one of the modes to which I have referred, the court will not give effect to it by applying another of those modes. If it is intended to take effect by transfer, the court will not hold the intended transfer to operate as a declaration of trust, for then every imperfect instrument would be made effectual by being converted into a perfect trust.'

In the case of land, an effectual transfer would be by conveyance; in the case of a debt by absolute written assignment thereof, whilst in the case of shares in a company by (1) a transfer in the form required by the company's articles, executed by the transferor, and (2) delivery of the transfer and share certificate to the transferee. Until the registration of the transfer by the company, the transferor is a trustee for the transferee. The directors may, under a power in the articles, refuse to register the transfer; if they so decline, then the transferor will continue as a trustee.

In *re Rose, Rose* v. *Inland Revenue Commissioners*[12] R, the registered owner of shares in the L.E. Company, executed, on 30 March 1943, a transfer of the shares in the form prescribed by the company's articles and delivered the transfer to the transferee, who thereupon executed the transfer. The transfer was registered by the company on 30 June 1943. R died more than five years after 30 March 1943, but less than five years after the registration of the transfer. The Crown claimed estate duty on a gift *inter vivos* of the shares, contending that the date of registration was the governing date. It was held, that the transfer was valid and effectual in equity from 30 March 1943, and accordingly the shares were not assessable to estate duty.

Under the Stock Transfer Act, 1963, a transfer of stock or shares does not require to be executed by the transferee. It is therefore suggested, in order that the transfer may be effectual to perfect a gift, that an acceptance clause in the form:

'I the above-named transferee hereby accept the transfer of the above security into my name'

be written into the Stock Transfer Form prescribed by the Act immediately below the name and address of the transferee, and signed by the transferee.

Coming back to trusts for valuable consideration, it should be made

[12] [1952] Ch. 499.

clear that natural love and affection is good, but is not valuable, consideration. Whilst if the intended beneficiary is not regarded as a volunteer, because he is within the marriage consideration it is necessary to enquire who is within such consideration. The answer is the parties to the marriage and their issue. Any one outside this class is a volunteer.

A gift in consideration of marriage is exempt from estate duty on the death of the donor, even if effected within five years of his death. The expression 'in consideration of marriage' should not be confused with 'within the marriage consideration.'

Consider the following cases:

(a) A on the occasion of his own marriage, makes a settlement of property. Here there is no element of gift, the settlement being made 'for the most valuable consideration imaginable, that of marriage.'[13]

(b) C on the occasion of his daughter's marriage to F settles £100,000 on trust for the benefit of the following objects, namely, his daughter, her husband, their issue and the settlor's other five children. The gift would be exempt from estate duty as being in consideration of marriage[14] though some of the objects would not be within the marriage consideration.

The rule that equity will not assist a volunteer is subject to a number of exceptions, and reference should be made to one or other of the standard works on the subject if information in regard to them is required.

(5) PROTECTIVE AND DISCRETIONARY TRUSTS

Any attempt to restrict the power of alienation, whether applied to an absolute interest in property or to a life estate therein is void, as being inconsistent with the interest given;[15] but a proviso determining the life interest expressed to be given, coupled with a gift over in the event of alienation or bankruptcy does not offend the rule just stated.

So that property may be given to a man *until* he shall become bankrupt. This is an effectual limitation, but if a life interest was expressed to be subject to a condition that it was not to be alienated, such condition would be void.[16]

If a life interest is effectively determined, a forfeiture is said to take effect, and provisions bringing this about are referred to as protective trusts.

---

[13] *Per* Kay, L.J., in *Att-General* v. *Jacobs Smith*, [1895] 2 Q.B. 341, 354.
[14] *Inland Revenue Commissioners* v. *Rennell*, [1963] 2 W.L.R. 745; but *see* Finance Act, 1963, s.53, and as regards deaths after 19 March 1968, Finance Act, 1968.
[15] *Rochford* v. *Hackman* (1852) 9 Hare 475.
[16] *Brandon* v. *Robinson* (1811) 18 Ves. 429.

Section 33 of the Trustee Act, 1925, provides:

(1) Where any income, including an annuity or other periodical income payment, is directed to be held on protective trusts for the benefit of any person (in this section called "the principal beneficiary") for the period of his life or for any less period, then, during that period (in this section called the "trust period") the said income shall, without prejudice to any prior interest, be held on the following trusts, namely:—

   (i) Upon trust for the principal beneficiary during the trust period or until he, whether before or after the termination of any prior interest, does or attempts to do or suffers any act or thing, or until any event happens, other than an advance under any statutory or express power, whereby, if the said income were payable during the trust period to the principal beneficiary absolutely during that period, he would be deprived of the right to receive the same or any part thereof, in any of which cases, as well as on the termination of the trust period, whichever first happens, this trust of the said income shall fail or determine;

   (ii) If the trust aforesaid fails or determines during the subsistence of the trust period, then, during the residue of that period, the said income shall be held upon trust for the application thereof for the maintenance or support, or otherwise for the benefit, of all or any one or more exclusively of the other or others of the following persons (that is to say)—

      (a) the principal beneficiary and his or her wife or husband, if any, and his or her children or more remote issue, if any; or

      (b) if there is no wife or husband or issue of the principal beneficiary in existence, the principal beneficiary and the persons who would, if he were actually dead, be entitled to the trust property or the income thereof or to the annuity fund, if any, or arrears of the annuity, as the case may be;

     as the trustees in their absolute discretion, without being liable to account for the exercise of such discretion, think fit.

(2) This section does not apply to trusts coming into operation before the commencement of this Act, and has effect subject to any variation of the implied trusts aforesaid contained in the instrument creating the trust.

(3) Nothing in this section operates to validate any trust which would, if contained in the instrument creating the trust, be liable to be set aside.

Discretionary trusts can arise independently of protective trusts and have in recent years been frequently created to minimise the charge to estate duty and surtax.

So long as there are more than two of the discretionary objects surviving, none has a right enforceable at law or in equity under the trust. When the number is reduced to two, and one of these two die, then and only then can there be a charge to estate duty. With one surviving object, the discretionary trust has come to an end and the trustees must apply the whole income (and may be the capital) for his benefit.

If a large majority of the shares of a family company are put into a discretionary trust, it will be practically impossible for the Inland Revenue to make an effective direction under section 245, Income Tax Act, 1952,[17] that the undistributed income of the company be apportioned among its members.

Certain precautions should be taken if these trusts are to be effective. For instance:

(a) The trustees must have an absolute discretion.

(b) Neither the settlor nor his spouse should be objects of the discretion.

(c) For the reason stated above the greater the number of objects the better.

Although there is no life interest in such a trust, for purpose of capital gains tax a life interest is deemed to have been determined every fifteen years.[18]

(B) EXPRESS PUBLIC TRUSTS—CHARITIES

(1) INTRODUCTION

In law charitable institutions enjoy rare and increasing privileges.[19] For instance, under sections 447 and 448, Income Tax Act, 1952, the income of charities is exempt from income tax, whilst if a charitable institution carries on a trade in furtherance of its objects, the profits therefrom are exempt from tax. Exemption from capital gains tax is given under section 35, Finance Act, 1965, and there are various other exemptions (total or partial) from estate duty, stamp duty and selective employment tax.

A reasonably clear idea of the scope of charity is therefore essential, but before examining this, two points of difference between private and charitable trusts should be noticed. In the case of express private trusts:

(a) there must be a beneficiary who can enforce the trust and

(b) the trust created must not offend the rule against perpetuities;[20] whilst in the case of charitable trusts:

(a) there is no certainty in regard to the beneficiaries; so that enforcement is by means of an action brought in the name of the Attorney-General, and

(b) provided the trust is limited to commence within the time allowed by the rule against perpetuities, it is valid though the objects are perpetual.

---

17 *See* as from 6 April 1966, section 78, Finance Act, 1965, relating to close companies.
18 Finance Act, 1965, s.25 (13).
19 *Per* Lord Simonds in *Oppenheim* v. *Tobacco Securities Trust Co. Ltd*, [1951] A.C. 297.
20 *See* Appendix A for a statement of this rule.

(2) MEANING OF CHARITY

' "Charity" in its legal sense[21] comprises four principal divisions:

(a) trusts for relief of poverty;

(b) trusts for the advancement of education;

(c) trusts for the advancement of religion;

(d) trusts for other purposes beneficial to the community, not falling under any of the preceding heads.'[22]

In making this classification, Lord Macnaghton added that the trusts in the fourth division 'are not the less charitable in the eye of the law because incidentally they benefit the rich as well as the poor, as indeed every charity that deserves the name must do either directly or indirectly.'

'To ascertain whether a gift constitutes a valid charitable trust so as to escape being void on the ground of perpetuity, a first enquiry must be whether it is public—whether it is for the benefit of the community or of an appreciably important class of the community. The inhabitants of a parish or town, or any particular class of such inhabitants, may for instance be the objects of such a gift, but private individuals, or a fluctuating body of private individuals cannot'[23] but the 'public test' is not applicable to trusts for the relief of poverty.[24]

Before considering Lord Macnaghton's four divisions, it should be stated that, if property bequeathed by will might consistently with the will, be applied to other than strictly charitable purposes, the trust would be too indefinite for the court to execute.[25] So a residuary bequest 'for such charitable institutions or other charitable or benevolent objects as my executors might select' would be void for uncertainty.[26]

The four divisions set out above will now be considered in some detail.

(a) Relief of Poverty

Trusts or gifts for the relief of poverty have been held to be charitable even though they are limited in their application to an aggregate of individuals

---

[21] That is to say 'in a sense or manner within the intendment of the preamble to the statute 43 Eliz. I c.4', per Lord Wilberforce in *Scottish Burial Reform and Cremation Society* v. *Glasgow Corporation*, [1967] 3 W.L.R. 1132, 1141, where it was held that cremation was for the public benefit within the intendment of that preamble.

[22] *Per* Lord Macnaghton in *Commissioners of Income Tax* v. *Pemsel*, [1891] A.C. 531, 583.

[23] *Per* Lord Wrenbury in *Verge* v. *Somerville*, [1924] A.C. 499.

[24] *See* under trusts for relief of poverty, *infra.*

[25] *James* v. *Allen* (1817) 3 Mer. 17. But a gift which is expressed to be for charitable as well as non-charitable purposes *may* be saved in the case of trusts created before 16 December 1952 by the Charitable Trusts (Validation) Act, 1954.

[26] *Chichester Diocesan Fund and Board of Finance (Incorporated)* v. *Simpson*, [1944] A.C. 341, affirming the decision of the Court of Appeal, reported *sub nom. In re Diplock*, [1941] 1 Ch. 253.

ascertained by reference to some personal tie (e.g. of blood or contract), such as the relations of a particular individual, the members of a particular family, the employees of a particular firm, the members of a particular association.[27]

Such trusts are therefore valid though they are not 'public' in the sense this word was used by Lord Wrenbury in *Verge* v. *Somerville*. Accordingly a trust for the relief of poverty amongst the employees of a particular company or their dependants is valid as a charitable trust.[28] Relief of the poor 'seems to connote need of some sort, either need for a home or the means to provide for some necessity or *quasi* necessity, and not merely an amusement however healthy it is.'[29]

(b) Advancement of Education

Education is not limited to subjects taught at schools and universities, but extends to provision for the study of cultural arts,[30] if it is for the public benefit, but if one of the purposes of the institution is to promote lectures which were simply propaganda for a political party, the purpose would not be regarded as charitable.[31] A gift for the education of descendants of named individuals is regarded as a family trust and not as one for the benefit of a section of the community.[32]

(c) Advancement of Religion

Here in order to come under this heading and so qualify as a legal charity the trust must be (1) for a strictly religious purpose, and (2) for the benefit of the public or a section of it.

In *Gilmour* v. *Coats*[33] a sum of money was declared to be held in trust to apply the income to the purposes of a certain Roman Catholic Priory, which consisted of a community of cloistered nuns who devoted their lives to prayer and contemplation within their convent but engaged in no exterior work. Here the purpose of the trust was a strictly religious one, but the element of public benefit, which is essential to render the purpose charitable in law, was absent.

(d) Other Charitable Purposes

Public benefit is implicit in Lord Macnaghton's fourth division, but in order to be charitable in law the trust must also be one the administration

[27] *Per* Jenkins, L.J., in *In re Scarisbrick*, [1951] 1 Ch. 622.
[28] *Gibson* v. *South American Stores (Gath & Chaves) Ltd*, [1950] Ch. 177.
[29] *Per* Harman, J., in *Baddeley* v. *C.I.R.*, [1955] 35 T.C. 661, 666 and approved by Lord Simonds at p. 696.
[30] *Royal Choral Society* v. *C.I.R.*, [1943] 25 T.C. 263; *In re Shakespeare Memorial Trust*, [1923] 2 Ch. 398.
[31] *Bonar Law Memorial Trust* v. *C.I.R.* (1933) 49 T.L.R. 220.
[32] *In re Compton*, [1945] Ch. 123.
[33] [1949] A.C. 426.

of which the Court could if necessary undertake and control. On these two grounds, it was held that a trust to establish a college for the training of mediums was invalid.[34] So a trust for the attainment of political objects has always been held invalid, not because it is illegal, but because the Court has no means of judging whether a proposed change in the law will or will not be for the public benefit.[35] However desirable the change may really be, the law could not stultify itself by holding that it was for the public benefit that the law itself should be changed.[36]

The general improvement of agriculture is a charitable purpose falling within this fourth division.[37]

As to trusts for the provision of facilities for recreation in the interests of social welfare, see The Recreational Charities Act, 1958, which was enacted following the decision of the House of Lords in *C.I.R.* v. *Baddeley*[38] that a trust to provide facilities for religious, social and physical training and recreation was not for charitable purposes only.

(3) THE CY-PRÈS DOCTRINE

This doctrine was explained by Kay, J., in his judgment in *In re Taylor*[39] in these words:

'If upon the whole scope and intent of the will you discover the paramount object of the testator was to benefit not a particular institution, but to effect a particular form of charity independently of any special institution or mode, then, although he may have indicated the mode in which he desires that to be carried out, you are to regard the primary paramount intention chiefly, and if the particular mode for any reason fails, the Court, if it sees a sufficient expression of a general intention of charity, will to use the phrase familiar to us, execute that *cy-près*, that is, carry out the general paramount intention indicated without which his intention itself cannot be effectuated.'

(C) TRUSTS OF IMPERFECT OBLIGATION

Normally a gift on trust must have a beneficiary, who can enforce the obligation (one of the three certainties noted earlier in this chapter) but there is 'a group of cases relating to horses and dogs, graves and monuments

---

[34] *In re Hummeltenburg*, [1923] 1 Ch. 237.
[35] *Bowman* v. *Secular Society Ltd*, [1917] A.C. 406; *National Anti-Vivisection Society* v. *C.I.R.*, [1947] A.C. 31.
[36] *Tyssen on Charitable Bequests*.
[37] *C.I.R.* v. *Yorkshire Agricultural Society*, [1928] 13 T.C. 58.
[38] [1955] A.C. 572; 35 T.C. 661.
[39] (1888) 58 L.T 538; *see also* the Charities Act, 1960, s.13, as to settling schemes under this doctrine.

—matters arising under wills and intimately connected with the deceased—in which the Courts have found means of escape'[40] from this rule. These trusts are usually referred to as trusts of imperfect obligation, being for a non-charitable beneficiary who cannot enforce it, though the trust may be enforced indirectly.

They are admittedly anomalous, are unlikely to be extended, and must be for a period not exceeding the perpetuity period.

As an example of the means of escape found by the Court, the case of *In re Thompson*[41] may be cited. There the testator bequeathed a legacy of £1,000 to a friend to be applied by him, in such manner as he should think fit towards the promotion and furtherance of foxhunting and devised and bequeathed his residuary estate to a Cambridge college. On the friend giving an undertaking to apply the legacy when received by him towards the objects expressed in the testator's will, Clauson, J., held 'in effect, that there was somebody who could enforce the purpose indicated because the college, as residuary legatees, would be entitled to the legacy but for the trust for its application, and they could apply to the Court to prevent any misapplication or breach of the undertaking'[42] given by the friend. *Quaere,* would this non-charitable trust have been held valid, if there had been no residuary legatee.

[40] *Per* Roxburgh, J., in *In re Astor's Settlement Trusts,* [1952] Ch. 534.
[41] [1934] Ch. 342.
[42] *In re Astor's Settlement Trusts, supra.*

4 Trusts Created by Operation of Law

(A) RESULTING TRUSTS

IN certain circumstances the trust property reverts to the settlor in which case there is said to be a resulting trust in his favour.

Cases in which there is a resulting trust are:

(1) FAILURE OF AN EXPRESS TRUST

Failure of consideration may occasion a resulting trust in favour of the settlor. Take the case of *In re Ames' Settlement*.[1] There A covenanted to transfer to trustees within one year of his son's marriage to F certain funds to be held on the usual trusts of a marriage settlement, the son taking the first life interest. After the transfer the marriage was declared to be a nullity. F subsequently remarried and released all her interests under the settlement. Consequently there was a complete failure of consideration for the covenant, and a resulting trust was declared in favour of the settlor.

Other cases of resulting trust occur where the failure is due to the perpetuity rule,[2] uncertainty, impossibility, or illegality. Where an appeal was made for subscriptions to a fund to rebuild the Queens Hall, London, (destroyed by enemy action) as a memorial to Sir Henry Wood, the founder of the Promenade Concerts, but it was impossible to carry out this perfectly good charitable object through insufficient support, it was held that there was a resulting trust for the subscribers.[3]

(2) FAILURE TO EXHAUST THE BENEFICIAL INTEREST

An example of this class of failure is *In re Abbott*[4] referred to by Harman, J., in *In re Gillingham Bus Disaster Fund*[5] in these words:

'A fund had been subscribed for the relief of two distressed old ladies who had been defrauded of their patrimony. There was no instrument of trust. When

---

[1] [1946] Ch. 217.
[2] *See* Appendix A for a statement of this rule.
[3] *In re Henry Wood National Memorial Trust, The Times,* 28 October 1965.
[4] [1900] 2 Ch. 326.
[5] [1958] Ch. 300.

4

the survivor of them died the trustees had not expended the whole of the moneys subscribed and the summons asked whether this surplus resulted to the subscribers or whether it was payable to the personal representatives of the two ladies.'

Here there was a trust *for a particular purpose* only and as this particular had not exhausted the trust fund there was a resulting trust to the subscribers.

Compare this with a bequest of a legacy of stock subject to the payment of an annuity to Y. This is an example of a gift *subject to the performance of a particular purpose*. As the gift is not limited to this particular purpose only, the donee on the completion of the performance, takes the resultant fund beneficially.

(3) PURCHASE IN THE NAME OF ANOTHER

'Where a man buys land in another's name, and pays money, it will be in trust for him that pays the money, tho' no deed declaring the trust, for the statute of 29 Car. 2, called the Statute of Frauds,[6] doth not extend to trusts raised by operation of law'.[7]

If property (real or personal) is purchased by A and put in the name of B, there is a resulting trust in favour of the purchaser A.

Exceptions:

(a) If B is a child or one to whom the purchaser then stood *in loco parentis*, there is no such resulting trust but a presumption of advancement.

(b) If B is the wife of A there is also a presumption of advancement.

These presumptions may be rebutted. In *Shephard* v. *Cartwright*[8] Lord Simonds quoted the following passage from *Snell's Equity*, 24th ed., p. 153,[9] when considering by what evidence the presumption can be rebutted:

'The acts and declarations of the parties before or at the time of the purchase, or so immediately after it as to constitute a part of the transaction, are admissible in evidence either for or against the party who did the act or made the declaration . . . But subsequent declarations are admissible as evidence only against the party who made them, and not in his favour.'

For other cases in which a resulting trust may arise such as (i) purchase by one in joint names of himself and another and (ii) joint purchase in name of one, reference should be made to *Nathan's Equity through the Cases*, 4th ed., p. 425, where the various cases are considered in detail.

[6] Now section 53 (1), Law of Property Act, 1925.
[7] *Anonymous* (1683) 2 Ventr. 361.
[8] [1955] A.C. 431, at p. 445.
[9] Now 26th ed., p. 195.

(B) CONSTRUCTIVE TRUSTS

In Chapter 2 it was noted that a constructive trust arises when the conduct and behaviour of a person in relation to property of which he is not an express trustee is such that the Court construes it as involving him in the duties and responsibilities of a trustee.

(1) SECRET TRUSTS

It will be in view that a testamentary instrument will be invalid unless it complies with the terms of section 9, Wills Act, 1937, as regards its execution.

The question to be considered under this heading is, will the Court in the exercise of its general equitable jurisdiction permit trusts not expressed in a testamentary instrument to be engrafted on bequests or devises made by the testator? This question must be considered under two headings, namely, fully secret trusts and half secret trusts.

(a) Fully secret trusts

Here neither the existence of the trust nor the terms thereof are disclosed by the will or codicil. Wood, V.-C., in *Wallgrave* v. *Tebbs*[10] explained these trusts thus:

'Where a person, knowing that a testator in making a disposition in his favour intends it to be applied for purposes other than his own benefit, either expressly promises, or by silence implies, that he will carry the testator's intention into effect, and the property is left to him upon the faith of that promise or undertaking, it is in effect a case of trust; and, in such a case, the Court will not allow the devisee to set up . . . the Statute of Wills . . . and for this reason; the devisee by his conduct has induced the testator to leave him the property, and, as Turner, L.J. says in *Russell* v. *Jackson*,[11] no one can doubt, that, if the devisee had stated that he would not carry into effect the intentions of the testator, the disposition in his favour would not have been found in the will. But in this the Court does not violate the spirit of the Statute; but for the same end, namely, prevention of fraud, it engrafts the trust on the devise, by admitting evidence which the Statute would in terms exclude, in order to prevent a party from applying property to a purpose foreign to that for which he undertook to hold it.'

In the case of a fully secret trust communication and acquiescence may be either before or after the execution of the will.[12]

(b) Half Secret Trusts

Here the existence of the trust is disclosed by the will or codicil, but the

---

[10] (1855) 2 K. & J. 313.
[11] (1852) 10 Ha. 204.
[12] *Moss* v. *Cooper* (1861) 1 J. & H. 352.

terms are not. *Blackwell* v. *Blackwell*[13] is the leading example of such trusts. There the testator by a codicil, bequeathed a legacy of £12,000 to five persons upon trust to invest according to their discretion and to 'apply the income for the purposes indicated by me to them'. Before the execution of the codicil the objects of the trust were communicated in outline to four of the legatees and in detail to the fifth, and the trust was accepted by all of them. The legatee to whom the communication had been made in detail also made a memorandum, on the same day, but shortly after the execution of the codicil, of the testator's instructions. The residuary legatees claimed a declaration that no valid trust had been created in favour of the objects communicated to the five persons principally on the ground that parol evidence could not be admitted to establish the purposes indicated by the testator, but the Judge of first instance held that the evidence was admissible, and proved a valid secret trust, and his decision was upheld in the Court of Appeal and the House of Lords.

In the case of a half secret trust communication and acquiescence must be before the execution of the will, since the trust has been disclosed in the will. To admit evidence of communication of the terms of the trust made after the execution of the will would be a contravention of the Wills Act.[14]

To summarise, the necessary elements to support secret trusts are:

(i) Intention of the testator.
(ii) Communication to the legatee.
(iii) Acquiescence by him, expressly or by implication.

In the case of fully secret trusts communication can be either before or after the execution of the will, whilst in the case of half secret trusts it must be *before* execution.

The fact that one of the objects of the secret trust was also one of the witnesses of the will does not deprive him of the benefit conferred by the secret trust.[15]

(2) VENDOR AS CONSTRUCTIVE TRUSTEE

If A, by a specifically enforceable contract, agrees to sell land to B, then immediately the contract is signed, A becomes a trustee of the land for B who obtains an equitable estate in the land, subject to A's lien for the balance of the purchase consideration. If A dies before completion, what passes on his death for purpose of estate duty is his lien, which is personalty, whilst if B dies before completion what passes on his death in his equitable estate in the land subject to the vendor's lien, that is realty.

[13] [1929] A.C. 318.
[14] *In re Keen*, [1937] Ch. 236.
[15] *In re Young*, [1951] Ch. 344.

(3) OTHER INSTANCES

Equity has always regarded a professional adviser whether he be solicitor, accountant, stockbroker or estate agent, and his client as being in a fiduciary relationship. So if the professional adviser whilst holding his client's money, places it on deposit with a bank, earning interest, the professional adviser is regarded as a constructive trustee of such profit.[16]

A member of the committee of inspection in the winding up of a company under the Companies Act, 1948, is in a fiduciary position. By the Winding Up Rules he is prohibited from purchasing from the liquidator any of the assets of the company. If in contravention of these rules he unwittingly purchases any such assets he is regarded as a constructive trustee of any profit he makes.[17]

[16] *Brown* v. *C.I.R.*, [1964] 3 W.L.R. 511, 521; *see also* the Solicitors Act, 1965.
[17] *In re Bulmer, ex parte Greaves*, [1937] Ch. 499, a case in bankruptcy where the rule is the same.

5 Void and Voidable Trusts

CERTAIN instances of void or voidable trusts have been given in earlier chapters. A summary of the principal instances are, for convenience of reference, listed below.

(A) VOID TRUSTS

(1) Those for a purpose contrary to public policy and therefore illegal, e.g.

    (a) For the benefit of future illegitimate children.
    (b) In consideration of future immoral relations.
    (c) In restraint of marriage.
    (d) Imposing a restraint on alienation.[1]

(2) Trusts contravening the rules against perpetuities and accumulations.[2]
(3) Trusts void for uncertainty.

Uncertainty in this sense arises, not by reason of the fact that the trusts of an instrument are obscure or difficult of interpretation—that is a difficulty which can be cured by a court of construction—but because, even when interpreted, the trusts are such that the Court cannot execute them.[3]

For example, where charitable purposes are mixed up with other purposes of such a shadowy and indefinite nature that the Court cannot execute them, or where the description includes purposes which may or may not be charitable and a discretion is vested in the trustees, the whole gift fails for uncertainty.[4]

(B) VOIDABLE TRUSTS

(1) In case of mistake of such a kind that it was not the deliberate act of a person understanding sufficiently the nature of what he was doing.[5]

[1] See p. 14.
[2] See Appendix A.
[3] Per Pennycuik, J., in Muir v. C.I.R., [1966] 1 W.L.R. 251 at p. 265.
[4] Blair v. Duncan, [1902] A.C. 37.
[5] Hall v. Hall (1873) 8 Ch. 430, 437.

(2) In cases of duress or undue influence.

There is a presumption of undue influence in certain relationships, e.g.

    (*a*) Guardian and Ward

    (*b*) Solicitor and client

    (*c*) Medical adviser

but undue influence may be proved as a fact.

(3) A settlement by an infant of an equitable interest in property is voidable by him within a reasonable time after attaining his majority.

(4) Under Law of Property Act, 1925, section 172, every conveyance of property made with intent to defraud creditors is voidable at the instance of any person thereby prejudiced.

(5) The Bankruptcy Act, 1914, section 42(1), provides that a voluntary settlement of property may be avoided if within two years of the date of the settlement, the settlor becomes bankrupt, whether it was fraudulent or not. Further if the settlement was made more than two years before the bankruptcy, but within ten years thereof, the settlement may be avoided unless the parties claiming under the settlement can prove

    (*a*) that the settlor was at the date of the settlement able to pay all his debts without resort to the property settled, and

    (*b*) that his interest in that property passed to the trustee of the settlement.

The section refers to the settlement being void, but the Courts have interpreted this as meaning voidable.

In the cases (1), (2) and (3) under Voidable Trusts, the right to avoid may be lost by laches or acquiescence.

6 Administration of a Trust

(A) THE GENERAL DUTIES OF A TRUSTEE

THE first duty of a trustee is to effect a reduction of the trust property into possession. If he is an original trustee, the property put into the trust will normally be scheduled to the trust deed; if it is registered stocks and shares they should be transferred[1] into the name or names of the trustee or trustees. Bearer securities retained or taken as an investment by a trustee (not being a trust corporation) must until sold be deposited for safe custody with a bank for account of the trustee, and the income must be collected by such bank.[2] Similarly cash should be paid into a bank account in their joint names. It will be in view that the authority of trustees is joint for all classes of property, and the bank account should only be operated by the signatures of all the trustees.

If on the other hand the trust property consists of an equitable interest, the trustee should give immediate notice of his appointment to the person or persons in whom the legal estate is vested.

A trustee in relation to the trust property should act as a prudent man of business. He should therefore see that any property requiring to be covered by insurance is so covered and the policy is in the name of the trustee or trustees.

Trustee Act, 1925, section 19(1), reads:

A trustee may insure against loss or damage by fire any building or other insurable property to any amount, including the amount of any insurance already on foot, not exceeding three fourth parts of the full value of the building or property, and pay the premiums for such insurance out of the income thereof or out of the income of any other property subject to the same trusts without obtaining the consent of any person who may be entitled wholly or partly to such income.

In regard to his duties, the trustee must follow the directions contained in the trust deed, so far as they are capable of being followed. A distinction

---

[1] *See* p. 13 as to the precaution to be taken if transfer forms under the Stock Transfer Act, 1963, are used.
[2] Trustee Act, 1925, s.7. Under the Exchange Control Regulations bearer securities must be in the custody of Authorised Depositaries.

must be drawn between directions given to and powers conferred on trustees. The former must be followed, but powers normally are permissive. 'It is settled law that when a testator has given a pure discretion as to the exercise of a power, the court does not enforce the exercise of the power against the wish of the trustees, but it does prevent them exercising it improperly.'[3]

A trustee may delegate his office, either:

(1) under an express power given in the trust instrument, or
(2) under statutory power, e.g. the Trustee Act, 1925. Section 23 of the Act authorises trustees—

   (a) to employ and pay an agent such as solicitor, banker, stock-broker;
   (b) to appoint an agent or attorney for the purpose of selling and managing any property subject to the trust situate outside the United Kingdom;
   (c) to permit a solicitor, or in the case of a policy of insurance, also a banker to have custody of documents receipted by the trustee, for the purpose of collecting the money due.

Providing he acts in good faith and does not permit any agent so appointed to retain money longer than is reasonably necessary, the trustee is not responsible for any loss occasioned by the agent.

In private trusts, trustees must act unanimously in making decisions, whereas in charitable or public trusts they can act according to the vote of the majority, providing the majority are acting within the terms of the trust.[4]

(B) INVESTMENT OF TRUST FUNDS

A trustee in investing the funds in his charge must choose those investments which are:

(1) within the terms of his trust, or
(2) authorised by statute, i.e. the Trustee Act, 1925, or from 3 August 1961 the Trustee Investments Act, 1961,[5] hereinafter referred to as the 1961 Act.

'As a general rule the law requires of a trustee no higher degree of diligence in the execution of his office than a man of ordinary prudence would exercise

---

[3] *Per* Jessel, M.R., in *Tempest* v. *Lord Camoys* (1882) 21 Ch. D. 571.
[4] *Luke* v. *South Kensington Co.* (1879) 11 Ch. D. 121.
[5] The provisions of the 1961 Act are set out in Appendix B.

in the management of his own private affairs. Yet he is not allowed the same discretion in investing the moneys of the trust as if he were a person *sui juris* dealing with his own estate. Business men of ordinary prudence may, and frequently do, select investments which are more or less of a speculative character; but it is the duty of a trustee to confine himself to the class of investments which are permitted by the trust, and likewise to avoid all investments of that class which are attended with hazard. So, so long as he acts in the honest observance of these limitations, the general rule already stated will apply.'[6]

The statutory direction as to the duty of trustees in choosing investments is contained in section 6, sub-section (1), of the 1961 Act.

In the exercise of his powers of investment a trustee shall have regard:

(*a*) to the need for diversification of investments of the trust in so far as is appropriate to the circumstances of the trust;

(*b*) to the suitability to the trust of investments of the description of investment proposed and of the investment proposed as an investment of that description.

Section 1 of the 1961 Act empowers a trustee to invest any property in his hands in:

(I)   Narrower-range investments not requiring advice,

(II) Narrower-range investments requiring advice,[7]

(III) Wider-range investments,

whilst a trustee may not make or retain any wider-range investments unless the trust fund has been divided into two parts, viz. narrower-range part, and wider-range part, the parts being, subject to the provisions of the Act equal in value at the time of division.[8]

The three classes of investments are detailed in the First Schedule to the Act (*see* Appendix B), and it will be noticed that Part II of that Schedule permits investment in debentures issued in the United Kingdom, by a company incorporated in the United Kingdom, being debentures registered in the United Kingdom, whilst Part III permits investment in any shares issued in the United Kingdom by a company incorporated in the United Kingdom and recorded on registers maintained there.

---

[6] *Per* Lord Watson in *Learoyd* v. *Whiteley* (1887) 12 A.C. 727.

[7] Advice is the advice of a person who is reasonably believed by the trustee to be qualified by his ability in and practical experience of financial matters, 1961 Act, section 6 (4), but such advice does not cover the advice required as to the suitability of a loan on mortgage of freehold or leasehold property.

[8] ibid., s.2 (1).

A company to come within the two provisions just set out must be one:

(*a*) whose securities are quoted on a recognised stock exchange in the United Kingdon or in Belfast;

(*b*) with an issued paid up share capital of not less than one million pounds, and

(*c*) which has paid a dividend on all shares issued in each of the five years immediately preceding the calendar year in which the investment is made.

Thus having permitted a measure of investment in what are generally referred to as equities and having laid down the 50/50 value basis as between narrower-range and wider-range, the Act makes some complex provisions for maintaining that basis. These fall to be considered under:

(1) ADDITIONS (OR ACCRUALS)[9]

These are divided into two classes:

(*a*) Accruals, such as bonus shares, which must be treated as belonging to the part of the fund giving rise to the accrual.

(*b*) Property brought into the settlement, e.g. a marriage settlement, under a covenant relating to after acquired property. In such cases, the 50/50 basis must be maintained by apportionment or compensating transfer between the two funds.

(2) WITHDRAWALS

Section 2(4) states:

Where in the exercise of any power or duty of a trustee property falls to be taken out of the trust fund, nothing in this section shall restrict his discretion as to the choice of property to be taken out.

So if estate duty has to be paid on the fund, say on the death of a tenant for life, the trustee has an absolute discretion as to which investments he sells to provide the duty payable. If for example, the values of the narrower-range and wider-range parts are £4,050 each, and £1,350 estate duty is raised by selling investments in the narrower-range, then instead of the values of the two funds being 50/50, they will be 40/60.

The Second Schedule to the 1961 Act deals with what is termed 'special-range property'. This is best explained by an example. If shares in a company which do not qualify as wider-range investments are settled on trust for conversion and the trustees are given power to postpone conversion for

[9] ibid., s.2 (3).

such period as they in their absolute discretion think fit, then in effect the shares would be an authorised investment so long as the trustees postpone conversion, and under the 1961 Act would be classed as 'special-range property' which must be kept separate from the other investments in the trust fund. Section 4 of the Trustee Act, 1925, provides that a trustee shall not be liable for breach of trust by reason only of his continuing to hold an investment which has ceased to be an investment authorised by the trust instrument or by the general law. Any such investment whilst it is continued to be held is regarded for the purpose of the 1961 Act as 'special-range property'. The Second Schedule contains provisions dealing with the re-investment of the proceeds of conversion of 'special-range property', with a view to maintaining the ratios between the narrower-range part and the wider-range part.

The powers conferred by section 1 of the 1961 Act are in addition to and not in derogation from any power conferred otherwise than by the Act.[10]

Where trustees are authorised to invest 'in or upon such investments as to them may seem fit' this does not restrict them to the statutory range of investments.[11]

Except in the case of strict settlements governed by the Settled Land Act, 1925, or where land is held by trustees on trust for sale, in which case section 28, Law of Property Act, 1925, will apply,[12] the statutory range of investments does not include a power to invest in land, but on reference to Appendix B, it will be seen that clause 13 of Part II of the First Schedule to the 1961 Act gives power to invest in mortgages of freehold property in England and Wales or Northern Ireland and of leasehold property in those countries of which the unexpired term at the time of investment is not less than sixty years.

'The courts of equity in England have indicated and given effect to certain general principles for the guidance of trustees in lending money on the security of real estate. Thus it has been laid down that in the case of ordinary agricultural land the margin ought not to be less than one-third of its value; whereas in cases where the subject of the security derives its value from buildings erected upon the land, or its use for trade purposes, the margin ought not to be less than one-half. I do not think these have been laid down as hard and fast limits up to which trustees will be invariably safe, and beyond which they can never be in safety to lend, but as indicating the lowest margins which in ordinary circumstances a careful investor of trust funds ought to accept. It is manifest that in cases where the subjects of the security are exclusively or mainly used for the purpose of trade, no prudent investor can be in a position to judge of

---

[10] ibid., s.3 (1).
[11] *In re Harari's Settlement*, [1949] 1 All E.R. 430.
[12] These two instances are outside the scope of this book. If information is required in regard to them, reference should be made to one of the standard works given in the List of Works Cited at p. xxiii.

the amount of margin necessary to make a loan for a term of years reasonably secure, until he has ascertained not only their present market price, but their intrinsic value, apart from those trading considerations which give them a speculative and it may be a temporary value.'[13]

With these general principles in mind, the detailed matters to which the trustee must direct his attention before making an advance on mortgage, if he is to claim the protection of section 8, Trustee Act 1925,[14] may now be stated.

(i) He must obtain a report as to the value of the property made by a person whom he reasonably believes to be an able practical valuer.

(ii) Such valuer must be instructed and employed independently of any owner of the property, that is to say 'the valuer must be entitled to look for his remuneration to the person who employs him and on the other hand, must be responsible to that person and to that person only for the due performance of his duty as valuer.'[15]

(iii) The trustee is entitled to assume 'that when the expert is directed to report on the value of the property, he will discover for himself those circumstances which bear on its value and will make his valuation in accordance with those circumstances.'[16] The income it is producing is one of those circumstances.

(iv) It is the valuer's duty to advise the trustee not only as to the actual value of the property, but also as to what proportion of that value may with safety be advanced.[17] If he merely puts the value of the property at 50 per cent above the amount the proposed borrower has requested, then he is not doing his duty and his report is not such a report as was contemplated by the Act.

Trustee Act, 1925, section 8, reads:

(1) A trustee lending money on the security of any property on which he can properly lend shall not be chargeable with breach of trust by reason only of the proportion borne by the amount of the loan to the value of the property at the time when the loan was made, if it appears to the court—

(a) that in making the loan the trustee was acting upon a report as to the value of the property made by a person whom he reasonably believed to be an able practical surveyor or valuer instructed and employed independently or any owner of the property, whether such surveyor or valuer carried on business in the locality where the property is situate or elsewhere; and

---

[13] *Per* Lord Watson in *Learoyd* v. *Whiteley* (1887) 12 A.C. 727.
[14] *Infra.*
[15] *In re Solomon*, [1912] 1 Ch. 261, 281.
[16] ibid., 274.
[17] ibid., 282.

(*b*) that the amount of the loan does not exceed two third parts of the value of the property as stated in the report; and

(*c*) that the loan was made under the advice of the surveyor or valuer expressed in the report.

(2) A trustee lending money on the security of any leasehold property shall not be chargeable with breach of trust only upon the ground that in making such loan he dispensed either wholly or partly with the production or investigation of the lessor's title.

(3) A trustee shall not be chargeable with breach of trust only upon the ground that in effecting the purchase, or in lending money upon the security, of any property he has accepted a shorter title than the title which a purchaser is, in the absence of a special contract, entitled to require, if in the opinion of the court the title accepted be such as a person acting with prudence and caution would have accepted.

(4) This section applies to transfers of existing securities as well as to new securities and to investments made before as well as after the commencement of this Act.

(C) THE GRATUITOUS NATURE OF TRUSTEESHIP

As a general rule, a trustee must act gratuitously, and is not entitled to compensation for personal trouble and loss of time.[18]

The exceptions to this rule are:

(1) Where there is a charging clause in the trust instrument.
    Example:

Any trustee being an accountant solicitor or other person engaged in any profession or business shall be entitled to be paid all usual professional or proper charges for business transacted time expended and acts done by him or any partner of his in connection with the trusts hereof including acts which a trustee not being in any profession or business could have done personally.

These clauses are construed strictly and it is doubtful whether the above or similar clauses would entitle a trustee to share commission with a stockbroker making purchases or sales of investments on behalf of the trust. It will be in view that under the Rules of the London Stock Exchange the benefit of reduced rates of commission permitted in certain cases cannot be given if the broker is sharing his commission on the transaction.

(2) By agreement with the beneficiaries, provided they are all *sui juris* and absolutely entitled to the whole trust estate. Such agreements are looked upon with suspicion and beneficiaries before they enter into such agreements should be separately advised.

(3) The Public Trustee and Judicial Trustees are by statute entitled to charge fees according to the prescribed scale for acting in any trust. Other

[18] *Brocksopp* v. *Barnes* (1820) 5 Madd. 90.

trust corporations invariably insist on a charging clause being inserted in the trust instrument before being named therein as a trustee.

(4) By authority of the Court.

Under section 42, Trustee Act, 1925, where the court appoints a corporation other than the Public Trustee, to be a trustee either solely or jointly with another person, the court may authorise the corporation to charge such remuneration for its services as trustee as the court may think fit.

Also where a trustee has performed exceptional services which have brought substantial benefits to the trust estate, the court will award remuneration on a liberal scale.[19]

(5) By virtue of the Rule in *Cradock* v. *Piper*.[20]

A solicitor trustee is normally in no better position than a lay trustee in the matter of remuneration. If there is no charging clause he cannot be remunerated for acting professionally in the trust. An exception was established in the case of *Cradock* v. *Piper*[20] where a solicitor trustee acted in legal proceedings on behalf of himself and his co-trustee. This rule will not prevent the solicitor or his firm from receiving the usual costs if the costs of appearing for himself and his co-trustee have not increased the costs which would have been incurred if he had appeared for those co-trustees only.

Sometimes a solicitor, instead of undertaking the legal work for the trust himself, employs one of his partners to act. In *Clark* v. *Carlon*[21] it was held that a solicitor trustee may employ his partner individually to act as solicitor for himself and his co-trustees in the affairs of the trust and pay him the usual charges, provided that it has been expressly agreed between himself and his partner that he himself shall not participate in the profits or derive any benefit from the charges.

What has just been stated about the gratuitous nature of trusteeship is but a corollary of the 'well established and salutary rule of equity that a trustee may not make a profit out of his trust . . . The rule is thus stated by Lord Herschell in *Bray* v. *Ford*.[22] "It is an inflexible rule of a Court of Equity that a person in a fiduciary position . . . is not, unless otherwise expressly provided, entitled to make a profit; he is not allowed to put himself in a position where his interest and duty conflict." ' [23]

For example, where the solicitor to trustees and one of the beneficiaries under the trust, which held 8,000 out of 30,000 shares in a manufacturing company, with the consent and knowledge of two out of three trustees of the estate obtained valuable information from the company, carried out

[19] *Boardman* v. *Phipps*, [1965] 2 W.L.R. 839.
[20] (1850) 1 M. & G. 664.
[21] (1861) 30 L.J.C. 639.
[22] [1896] A.C. 51.
[23] *Per* Russell, J., in *Williams* v. *Barton*, [1927] 2 Ch. 9.

long and skilful negotiations and acquired 21,986 of the other 22,000 shares, whereby the trust's holding was enhanced in value and the solicitor and beneficiary themselves made a profit of some £75,000, the House of Lords, by a majority, held that though the two acted with complete honesty and their integrity was not in doubt, nevertheless they must account to the trust estate for their profit. They were, however, as mentioned earlier in this section, allowed remuneration for their services on a liberal scale.[24]

But where B a director of X company was appointed a director of Y company in which X held shares, and on some of these shares being transferred to him to provide his qualification required by the regulations of Y he executed a declaration of trust covering these shares, B was declared entitled to retain the remuneration paid to him by Y, on the ground that such remuneration was paid to him, not for acting as a trustee, but for carrying out his duties as a director.[25]

(D) DEALINGS WITH THE TRUST PROPERTY

In the course of his duties, a trustee may have to sell or divide the trust property, and certain rules have been laid down in connection with such transactions.

(1) A trustee should not purchase any of the property of which he is a trustee.[26] The same prohibition applies to a member of a committee of inspection in a bankruptcy. Neither the trustee nor any of the committee of inspection may purchase any of the property of the bankrupt. This follows from the rule that any one in a fiduciary position must not put himself in a position where his interest and duty conflict.

As a rule, if a trustee has to realise real estate, he should put it up to auction to ensure as far as possible that he obtains the best possible price. Here again he should not bid for the property, in order to avoid the charge that he has persuaded other persons not to bid.

For similar reasons, a trustee will be prevented from selling trust property to a company of which he is the principal shareholder,[27] or to a partnership of which he is a member.

(2) A trustee may buy from his *cestui que trust*, provided there is a distinct and clear contract, ascertained to be such after a jealous and scrupulous examination of all the circumstances, that the

---

[24] *Boardman* v. *Phipps*, [1966] 3 W.L.R. 1009.
[25] *In re Dover Coalfield Extension Ltd*, [1908] 1 Ch. 65.
[26] *Ex parte Lacey* (1802) 6 Ves. 625.
[27] *Silkstone & Haigh Moor Coal Co.* v. *Edey*, [1900] 1 Ch. 167.

cestui que trust intended the trustee should buy; and there is no fraud, no concealment, no advantage taken, by the trustee of information acquired by him in the character of trustee.[28]

(3) Trustees who hold property on trust for conversion and the division of the proceeds between a number of beneficiaries may agree with any beneficiary who has a vested interest to appropriate to his share a specific portion of the property and if at the time the appropriation was fair and reasonable, other beneficiaries who subsequently attain a vested interest in the fund cannot complain if there has been a fall in the value of the balance of the fund.[29]

The power of appropriation often has to be exercised on the determination of a life interest and where the trust fund includes stocks and shares, difficult questions may arise in regard to the treatment of dividends and interest accruing over a period that includes the date of the determination of the life interest. Certain rules have been formulated[30] for adjusting the rights between the parties. They are:

(*a*) Trust for sale on determination of life tenancy

No apportionment is permitted in favour of life tenant's estate where the stocks and shares are sold cum div.[31]

(*b*) Trust for division in specie on same event

(i) *Stocks and shares sold cum div. in due course of administration,* e.g. to meet estate duty.
No apportionment is made in favour of life tenant's estate.

(ii) *Stocks and shares divided in specie amongst the remaindermen, or sold cum div. either at their request or in order to facilitate division*
Representatives of life tenant are entitled to an apportioned part of any dividends paid on such stocks and shares in respect of a period in which the life tenant's death occurs.[32] If the stocks are sold cum div. in the circumstances stated, such sale would be made 'not in the execution of any trust or power for sale vested in the trustees.'[33]

(iii) *Trustees owing to stocks and shares not being divisible into aliquot parts exercise their powers of appropriation*
Here the life tenant's rights are the same as under (*b*) (ii), since

[28] *Per* Lord Eldon in *Coles* v. *Trecothick* (1804) 9 Ves. 246.
[29] *In re Lepine*, [1892] 1 Ch. 210. As to a personal representative's power of appropriation, *see* Administration of Estates Act, 1925, s.41.
[30] *See In re Henderson*; *Public Trustee* v. *Reddie*, [1940] 1 Ch. 368.
[31] *Scholefield* v. *Redfern* (1863) 2 Dr. & Sm. 173.
[32] *Bulkeley* v. *Stephens*, [1896] 2 Ch. 241.
[33] ibid., at p. 250.

5

any appropriation under the Administration of Estates Act, 1925, section 41, must be made according to the respective rights of the person interested in the fund.

It is a necessary corollary of these rules that in appropriating stocks and shares, the accrued interest in the cum div. price of stocks and shares must be eliminated; in other words, schemes of appropriation must be prepared on the bare capital values of the stocks and shares.

(E) TRUSTEE'S DUTY TO BE IMPARTIAL

Trustees in the administration of their trust must hold the scales evenly between the beneficiaries.[34] This duty can be illustrated under a number of headings.

(1) THE RULE IN *Howe* v. *Dartmouth*[35]

In many wills the testator gives his real and personal property to his personal representatives on trust to convert that part not consisting of authorised investments and then directs them out of the proceeds of conversion and of his ready money to pay his debts, testamentary expenses and legacies and to invest the balance in authorised securities which, together with those held at date of death, are to form his residuary estate to be held on trust for one or more persons for life with remainder over to others.

Here there is an express trust for conversion which must be carried out. In the case of unauthorised investments, whether they be hazardous, wasting or merely unauthorised, equity says that the rights of the beneficiaries are to be adjusted on the footing that that which ought to have been done has been done. There is a presumed intention of equality of enjoyment and this can only be attained by selling the hazardous and wasting assets, which may be producing a very high income, and investing the proceeds in authorised securities.

Frequently the testator gives the trustees a power to postpone conversion for such period as they in their absolute discretion think fit. They can thus time the conversion and so avoid having to realise unauthorised securities under very difficult market conditions. But trustees must address their mind to the problem and take a positive decision one way or the other.[36]

In the case of *Howe* v. *Dartmouth*,[35] there was no express trust for conversion, but on the presumed intention of the testator that there was to be

[34] *In re Brookes*, [1914] 1 Ch. 558.
[35] (1802) 7 Ves. 137.
[36] *See In re Heys Settlement Trusts*, [1945] Ch. 294.

equality of enjoyment of the residuary estate, a trust for conversion was implied.

The rule is:

> Where there is a residuary bequest of personal estate to be enjoyed by several persons in succession, a Court of Equity, in the absence of any evidence of a contrary intention, will assume that it was the intention of the testator that his legatees should enjoy the same thing in succession, and as the only means of giving effect to such intention, will direct the conversion into permanent investments of a recognised character of all such parts of the estate as are of a wasting or reversionary character, and also all such other existing investments as are not of the recognised character and are consequently deemed to be more or less hazardous.[37]

The following points should be noted. The rule is not applicable unless you find:

(1) A disposition by will. Settlements *inter-vivos* are not within the rule.
(2) The property settled is personalty. Realty is not within the rule.
(3) A residuary bequest for persons in succession. A specific legacy is not within the rule.
(4) Absence of any evidence that the testator intended the property to be enjoyed in specie.

The methods of adjustment can now be stated.

(*a*) Express or implied trust for conversion, with no power to postpone.

    (i) If the hazardous assets are sold within a year of death, the life tenant is entitled to notional interest at 4 per cent per annum on the net proceeds of sale from date of death to date of realisation.[38]

    (ii) In the case of those unconverted at the end of the year from date of death, the life tenant is entitled to 4 per cent per annum from date of death to date of conversion on their value at the end of the first year.[39]

(*b*) Express trust for conversion, with power to postpone for such period as the trustees in their absolute discretion think fit.

    (i) If conversion is effected within a year of death the adjustment is as stated in (*a*) (i) above.[40]

    (ii) If conversion not effected within the first year, the life tenant is entitled to 4 per cent per annum from date of death to date

---

[37] *Macdonald* v. *Irvine* (1878) 8 Ch. at p. 112.
[38] *Brown* v. *Gellatly* (1867) L.R. 2 Ch. 751.
[39] *Dimes* v. *Scott* (1827) 4 Russ. 195.
[40] *In re Berry*, [1962] Ch. 97.

of conversion on the value of the hazardous assets at the date of death.[41]

These rules of adjustment do not apply if the life tenant is entitled to enjoy the property in specie, i.e. in its existing state. The life tenant is so entitled in the following cases:

(1) Where the property is realty, unless a contrary intention is expressed.
(2) Since 1925, where the property is leasehold, as by virtue of section 28(2), Law of Property Act, 1925, the life tenant is entitled to the net rents, after paying the outgoings, of such property.[42]
(3) Where it plainly appears upon the whole context of the will that the testator's intention was that the life tenant should derive the same income from the residuary estate as he had himself derived from the property up to the period of his death.[43] For example:

(a) When a testator has directed that the conversion of his estate shall take place at some time other than that at which the rule of the Court would make conversion necessary, the rule of the Court has no application.[44] So where a testator directs that the conversion shall be effected on the death,[45] or subject to the consent[46] of the life tenant, the latter is entitled to enjoy the property in specie.
(b) A power to retain is strong evidence that the life tenant is entitled to enjoyment in specie.[47]

The income actually produced in excess of the notional income must be invested in authorised securities. In making the comparison between the actual and the notional income, the 4 per cent per annum is calculated on the aggregate of the unauthorised investments. Should in any year the actual income be less than the notional, the deficiency is carried forward and recouped out of:

(a) any excess income over the 4 per cent in future years, and
(b) any proceeds of sale of unauthorised securities subsequently realised.

But there must be a deficiency at the time such sources are available for recoupment. Once the surplus income or the proceeds of sale are invested

---

[41] *In re Parry*; *Brown* v. *Parry* (1947) 62 T.L.R. 543. The rate of interest allowed in this case was 4 per cent and there does not appear to have been any change since.
[42] *In re Brooker*, [1926] W.N. 93; *In re Berton*, [1939] Ch. 200.
[43] *Alcock* v. *Sloper* (1833) 2 My. & K. 699.
[44] *Per* North, J., in *In re Pitcairn*, [1896] 2 Ch. 199.
[45] *Alcock* v. *Sloper supra*.
[46] *In re Rogers*, [1915] 2 Ch. 437.
[47] *In re Bates*, [1907] 1 Ch. 22.

in authorised securities they cannot be used for recoupment. No apportionment under the Apportionment Act, 1870, is made at the date of death for the purpose of these calculations.[48]

Under the Administration of Estates Act, 1925, section 33(1), the estate of an intestate becomes subject to a trust for conversion, with a power to postpone, and if there are successive interests, the rule in *Howe* v. *Dartmouth* will apply.[49]

Whereas under this rule, unauthorised securities are converted for the benefit of the remainderman, reversionary interests should be converted for the benefit of the life tenant. If the trustees exercise their discretion to postpone conversion, then when the interest falls in, or is otherwise realised, the net proceeds are apportionable under the rule in *In re Chesterfield's Trust*,[50] by ascertaining the sum which put out at interest at 4 per cent per annum at the date of death of the testator and accumulating at compound interest at that rate with yearly rests and deducting income tax at the standard rate for the time being would with the accumulation of interest have produced, at the date of receipt, the amount actually received; the sum so ascertained is capital and the balance income.

The *Chesterfield Trust* rule does not apply to:

(*a*) Realty, or

(*b*) If the life tenant is entitled to enjoy the property forming the residuary estate in specie.

(2) THE RULE IN *Allhusen* v. *Whittell*[51]

It was pointed out in Chapter 1 that until the executors have completed the administration of their testator's estate, the residue does not come into existence, and accordingly the residuary legatees have no beneficial interest in the estate or the income arising therefrom during the period of administration. The income received is the executors' and is capital in their hands. If the residue is settled on persons in succession, does the life tenant get income in respect of this period? Sir Wilfrid Greene, M.R., gave the following explanation in *Corbett* v. *Commissioners of Inland Revenue*:[52]

'The *Allhusen* v. *Whittell* rule really exists to save the tenant for life from being prejudiced by the particular nature of the executor's interest and the particular status of the estate during administration . . . When the residue is settled, it does become necessary to dissect the sum which remains in the executors' hands at the conclusion of the administration, because if that were not done

[48] *In re Fawcett*, [1940] Ch. 402.
[49] *See* in *In re Fisher*, [1943] Ch. 377.
[50] (1883) 24 Ch. D. 643.
[51] L.R. 4 Eq. 295.
[52] 21 T.C. at p. 462.

the tenant for life would be prejudiced by the fact of administration, and the longer it took, the more he would be prejudiced. Equity then steps in and says "As between the tenant for life and the remainderman, we are going to impress for our own purpose a particular character on this fund. We are going to treat it, as between you two parties, as divisible in part to the tenant for life, and in part to the remainderman", and the principle on which it is divided is a principle which in effect throws upon the tenant for life the burden of the administration to this extent, that capital is treated as liable to contribute such a sum of capital as, with the income thereon for the relative period, would provide for the necessary expenses.[53] The effect of that adjustment is that the tenant for life, when he receives that sum, is receiving a sum equal to the income of the estate, less the income which that part of capital notionally applied would have produced . . . In my opinion, the existence of the rule in *Allhusen* v. *Whittell* cannot alter the fundamental fact that, during the period of administration, the income is the executors' income and nobody else's.'[54]

The following observations may be made:

(*a*) If Sir Wilfrid Greene's view is correct—it has not been controverted— then the practice sometimes adopted of inserting a clause in a will to the effect that the rule in *Allhusen* v. *Whittell* is not to apply may prejudice the life tenant.

(*b*) Extremely elaborate and minute calculations are not required when applying the rule.

(*c*) In many cases a fair and proper method of giving effect to the rule would be to debit to capital the outgoings for debts, expenses and legacies, together with interest on any such debts as carried interest (e.g. estate duty) and credit capital with the whole of the dividends received on the securities realised for payment of the outgoings.

(3) BONUS (OR SCRIP) ISSUES OF SHARES

When a company makes distribution to its shareholders it is necessary where shares in the company form part of a trust fund to determine whether, as between life tenant and remainderman, the distribution is to be treated as income or capital. The following rules, based on *Bouch* v. *Sproule*[55] and other decisions over the years, including Lord Russell of Killowen's judgment in *Hill* v. *Permanent Trustee Co. of New South Wales*,[56] may be formulated.

(*a*) A limited company, when it parts with moneys available for distribution among its shareholders is not concerned with the fate of those moneys in the hands of any shareholder.[57]

---

[53] i.e. debts, testamentary expenses and legacies.
[54] But as from 1938, *see* Income Tax Act, 1952, Part XIX.
[55] (1887) 12 App. Cas. 385.
[56] [1930] A.C. 720, 732.
[57] ibid.

(b) As a limited company's power of declaring dividends ceases at the commencement of the winding up, any distribution, whether of cash or shares, after the date of commencement of the liquidation must be treated as capital.[58]

(c) A limited company not in liquidation can make no payment by way of return of capital to its shareholders except:

   (i) as a step in an unauthorised reduction of capital,[59]

or (ii) under section 56, Companies Act, 1948, by making a payment to shareholders out of a share premium account.[60]

Any other payment by means of which it parts with money to its shareholders can only be by way of dividing profits, whether it be called 'dividend' or 'bonus' or by any other name.[61]

(d) If a company in the exercise of its power pays a sum as dividend, the money so paid in respect of any shares which are settled will, *prima facie*, belong to the person beneficially entitled to the income. This of course is subject to any provision to the contrary in the trust deed.[62]

The company may if empowered pay the dividend by distributing marketable investments that it holds among its assets, and such distribution will be treated in the same way as a cash distribution by way of dividend,[63] unless the purchase of the shares by the trustees was made with the consent of the life tenant after it became known that such a distribution in specie was to be made. In such circumstances the distribution falls to be treated as capital.[64]

(e) Other considerations arise when a company deals with undivided profits in such a way that no part of it leaves the possession of the company, but the whole is applied in paying up new shares, or debentures or loan stock issued by the company,[65] which are issued proportionately to the shareholders who would have been entitled to receive the fund had it been in fact distributed as dividend. Such new shares, debentures or loan stock are treated as an addition to the capital of the settled fund.[66]

[58] *In re Armitage*, [1893] 3 Ch. 337.
[59] *Hill* v. *Permanent Trustee Co. of N.S.W.*, *supra*.
[60] *In re Duff's Settlement*, [1951] 2 T.L.R. 474.
[61] *Hill* v. *Permanent Trustee Co. of N.S.W.*, *supra*.
[62] ibid.
[63] *In re Sechiari*, [1951] 1 All E.R. 417; *In re Kleinwort*, [1951] Ch. 860.
[64] *In re MacLaren*, [1951] 2 T.L.R. 209.
[65] *C.I.R.* v. *Fisher's Executors*, [1926] A.C. 395; *In re Outen*, [1963] Ch. 291.
[66] *Hill* v. *Permanent Trustee Co. of N.S.W.*, *supra*.

(f) Where an investment is, in accordance with the direction of the testator, set aside to form an appropriated fund to answer annuities, any bonus shares issued in respect of that investment belong to the appropriated fund and do not fall into the residue of the estate.[67]

(F) ACCOUNTS AND AUDIT

It is the duty of trustees to be constantly ready with accounts and un-justifiable refusal or neglect on the part of the trustees may entail them being charged with the expense occasioned.

Section 22(4), Trustee Act, 1925, makes provision for the trustees to have an audit of their accounts in the circumstances therein mentioned.

A beneficiary or beneficiaries may apply to the Public Trustee under section 13, Public Trustee Act, 1906, for an audit to be carried out by a solicitor or accountant. The practice of the Public Trustee is to try and persuade the parties to agree on the nomination of a person to undertake the audit. It is only if agreement cannot be reached by the parties that the Public Trustee makes an appointment under the section.

(G) MAINTENANCE AND ADVANCEMENT

When infants are beneficiaries under a trust their parents or guardians will often want to know whether any provision can be made for them either out of income for their maintenance, e.g. education, holidays and living expenses, or out of capital for their advancement, e.g. the purchase of a house on their marriage.

The first question is: have the trustees power to apply income towards the beneficiary's maintenance or capital towards his advancement? Such power may be given:

(a) by the trust instrument, or
(b) by statute.

The statutory provisions are contained in sections 31 and 32, Trustee Act, 1925, which only apply if and so far as a contrary intention is not expressed in the instrument creating the trust and have effect subject to the terms of the instrument.[68]

It should be noted that the statutory provisions now to be considered do not impose any duty on trustees; they merely give them *power* to apply money for maintenance or advancement.[69]

---

[67] *In re Street*, [1922] 67 S.J. 79.
[68] Trustee Act, 1925, s.69(2).
[69] *See In re Turner's Will Trusts*, [1937] Ch. 15.

(1) MAINTENANCE

Under section 31, where trustees hold property in trust for any person for any interest whatsoever, whether vested or contingent, they may at their sole discretion, during the infancy of such person pay to his parent or guardian or otherwise apply for or towards his maintenance, education or benefit the whole or such part of the income of that property whether or not there is:

(a) any other fund applicable to the same purpose; or

(b) any person bound by law to provide for his maintenance or education.

In deciding whether to exercise this *power* under section 31, the trustees are to have regard to:

(a) the age of the infant;

(b) generally to the circumstances of the case; and

(c) in particular to what other income is available for his maintenance.

If the infant's interest is a contingent one then the *power* under section 31 can only be exercised if the trust carries the intermediate income. This question must be considered under a number of headings.

(i) Contingent gift by will of residuary personalty.	Whether the will came into operation[70] before or after 1 January 1925, such gift carries the intermediate income.[71]
(ii) Contingent residuary devise of freehold land.	If will comes into operation after 1 January 1925, the gift carries the intermediate income it produces.[72]
(iii) Contingent specific devise of freehold land.	do.
(iv) Contingent specific legacy.	do.

A pecuniary legacy does not carry intermediate income unless the testator was the father of, or in *loco parentis* to, the infant legatee. If the legacy is contingent, the contingency must have reference to the infancy of the legatee. If interest is payable, the rate is 5 per cent per annum.

Any balance of income which is not used for the infant's maintenance must be accumulated, but the trustees may, at any time during the infancy of such person, if his interest so long continues, apply these accumulations as if they were income of the current year.[73]

---

[70] A will comes into operation when the testator dies.
[71] *In re Adams*, [1893] 1 Ch. 329.
[72] Law of Property Act, 1925, s.175.
[73] Trustee Act, 1925, s. 31(2).

When the infant beneficiary attains the age of twenty-one, or marries under that age, the trustees are to hold the accumulated income in trust for such person absolutely:

(a) if during his infancy or until his marriage his interest is a vested interest, or

(b) on those events he becomes entitled absolutely to the property producing the income,

always subject to any settlement made by him under any statutory powers during his infancy.[74]

In any other case, the trustees are to add the accumulations to the capital of the property so as to form one fund.

Trustees cannot apply income for a beneficiary's maintenance after he has reached the age of twenty-one, but must pay it to him until he either attains a vested interest or dies, or until his interest in the property fails.[75]

(2) ADVANCEMENT

Section 32, Trustee Act, 1925, gives trustees power to pay or apply any capital money subject to the trust for the advancement or benefit of any person entitled to the capital of the trust property or any share thereof, whether absolutely or contingently, and notwithstanding that the interest of that person may be defeated by the exercise of a power of appointment or diminished by the increase of the class to which it belongs.

The conditions governing the exercise of such power are:

(a) the amount advanced must not exceed altogether in amount one-half of the presumptive or vested share of that person in the trust property;

(b) if that person is or becomes absolutely and indefeasibly entitled to a share in the trust property, the amount advanced is to be treated as a payment on account of that share and brought in account, and

(c) if the making of the advance would prejudice any prior interest the consent of the person with that interest must consent to the advance being made.

'Benefit' is a word of 'very large import',[76] and the power of advancement can be exercised only if it is for the benefit of the infant that he should have a share of capital before his due time. Furthermore, trustees should take all reasonable steps to see that the advance is applied for the purpose for which it was made.[77]

[74] ibid.
[75] ibid., s.31(1) (ii).
[76] *In re Stranger*, [1891] 60 L.J. Ch. 327.
[77] *See In re Pauling*, [1964] Ch. 303.

The practice of trustees making an advance to a beneficiary which he immediately resettles for the benefit of himself and issue has been fairly common in recent years, and such sub-trusts will be upheld if for the real benefit of the beneficiary.[78]

Where trustees make an advance under section 32, Trustee Act, 1925, with the consent of the life tenant and the infant does not attain an absolute and indefeasible interest in the trust property, the trustees are not accountable for estate duty under the Finance Act, 1940, section 43.[79]

(H) INDEMNITY AND PROTECTION OF TRUSTEES

The duties of a trustee are onerous and therefore it is only right that he should be entitled to indemnity in the proper performance of his duties, and also to protection when distributing the trust fund.

The right of indemnity may be against:

(a) The trust estate, e.g. for solicitor's costs, calls on shares, etc.

(b) The beneficiary, e.g. where he is a sole beneficiary *sui juris* and entitled absolutely or where the liability was incurred at the request of the beneficiary.

Section 30, Trustee Act, 1925, provides that a trustee may reimburse himself or pay or discharge out of the trust premises all expenses incurred in or about the execution of the trusts and powers. But not if the expenses were improperly incurred through unreasonable conduct on the part of the trustee.[80]

Before distributing a trust estate, a trustee should:

(a) Obtain protection by means of advertisement, pursuant to section 27,[81] Trustee Act, 1925, in the *London Gazette*, and in a London daily, and also if there is land situate out of London, then in a local paper as well. Two months' notice at least should be given of the intention to distribute.

(b) If a beneficiary has assigned his interest in the fund, investigate such assignment. Care should have been taken that all notices of assignment by assignees were noted in the trust records when received.

(c) Have his accounts approved by the beneficiaries and take a discharge from them.

[78] *Pilkington* v. *C.I.R.*, [1964] A.C. 612.
[79] Finance Act, 1950, s.44(2).
[80] *In re Chapman*, [1895] L.T. 66.
[81] This section is applicable notwithstanding anything to the contrary in the instrument creating the trust.

7 Liability for Breach of Trust

(A) GENERAL TEST OF LIABILITY

A trustee is liable for breach of trust if he commits an act, or if he is in default, whereby the trust and the interest of the beneficiaries is prejudiced.[1]

For example one, Townley, joined, for conformity with his co-trustee in signing receipts for rents paid to the trust. He did not in fact receive any of the rents, but allowed them to remain in the hands of his co-trustee, who became insolvent. Townley did not incur any liability for having signed the receipts,[2] but was held liable for breach of trust in having left the rents in the hands of his co-trustee for an unreasonable time without enquiry, inasmuch this was an act which prejudiced the trust.

Further examples are:

(i) Investing trust funds in unauthorised investments.[3]

(ii) Omitting to see that investments are registered in the names of all the trustees.

(iii) Unreasonable delay in carrying out directions of the settlor whereby a loss is incurred.

(iv) Improper retention of unauthorised investments.[4]

(B) DEFAULT OF CO-TRUSTEE

The next question is: to what extent, if any, is a trustee liable for the acts or default of his co-trustee? In the following cases it would appear that he is so liable.

(i) If he allows trust funds to remain under the sole control of his co-trustee.[5]

(ii) If he leaves the conduct of the trust to his co-trustee without interesting himself in the matter.[6]

---

[1] *Townley* v. *Sherborne* (1634) Bridge J. 35.
[2] *See* s.30(1) Trustee Act, 1925, *post.*
[3] *Knott* v. *Cottee* (1852) 16 Beav. 77.
[4] *Fry* v. *Fry* (1859) 27 Beav. 144.
[5] *Townley* v. *Sherborne, supra.*
[6] *Chambers* v. *Minchin* (1802) 7 Ves. 186.

(iii) If he stands by aware of facts that should inform him that his co-trustee is committing or is about to commit, a breach of trust, since it is the duty of a trustee 'to watch over, and if necessary, to correct the conduct of each other'.[7]

Once it is determined that there has been a breach of trust then the liability of the trustees is joint and several; in other words the beneficiaries may call on any two or more of the trustees jointly or any one of them separately. Normally there would be a right of contribution, that is to say the liability must be shared. But in the following cases the Court may treat the co-trustee as solely liable:

(i) where the trustee acted under the guidance of his solicitor trustee;[8]
(ii) where the co-trustee has himself obtained the benefit of the breach of trust.

In those or similar cases the trustee has a right of indemnity against his co-trustee.

Trustee Act, 1925, section 30 (1), reads:

A trustee shall be chargeable only for money and securities actually received by him notwithstanding his signing any receipt for the sake of conformity and shall be answerable and accountable only for his own acts, receipts, neglects or defaults, and not for any banker, broker or other person with whom any trust money or securities may be deposited, nor for the insufficiency or deficiency of any securities, nor for any other loss, unless the same happens through his own wilful default.

'Wilful default' has been interpreted as meaning 'either a consciousness of negligence or breach of duty, or a recklessness in the performance of a duty.'[9]

(C) EXTENT OF LIABILITY

In general the remedy for breach of trust is to compensate the trust for the loss suffered, or to recover from the trustee any unauthorised profit he has made. If there is neither loss to the capital of the trust, nor a profit to the trustee by the breach of trust, then there is no liability.[10]

Take the case of a trustee improperly realising an authorised security, the proceeds amounting to £500. If to purchase the same amount of stock would now cost £550, the beneficiary is entitled to call on the trustee to

[7] *Per* Lord Cottenham in *Styles* v. *Guy* (1849) 1 M. & G. 422, 433.
[8] *In re Partington* (1887) 57 L.T. 654.
[9] *Per* Maugham, J., in *In re Vickery*, [1931] 1 Ch. 572.
[10] *Per* Cozens-Hardy, M.R., in *Slade* v. *Chaine*, [1908] 1 Ch. 522.

replace the stock and bear the cost of doing so. If on the other hand the particular stock has fallen in value and could be replaced at a cost of £450, the beneficiary can either call on the trustee to repurchase the stock at his expense or refund to the trust the proceeds, viz. £500. Some interest adjustment in favour of a life tenant may also be required, depending on the circumstances.

If interest is payable by a trustee in default, the Court may, if the trustee has been guilty of wilful default, increase the rate of interest to show its displeasure at his conduct.

(D) IMPOUNDING BENEFICIARY'S INTEREST

If a trustee who is in default is also a beneficiary of the trust, his interest as a beneficiary can be impounded until the default has been made good. This rule applies whether his beneficial interest is original or derivative. For example X and Y are beneficiaries of a trust, of which A is the trustee. On X's death, A, the trustee, succeeds under the intestacy or will of X to the latter's share. A's derivative interest can be impounded if, in his capacity as trustee, he is in default.[11]

An assignee of the trustee's beneficial interest takes subject to this equity available to the trust estate. This is so even if the default of the trustee occurs after he has assigned his beneficial interest.[12]

If a trustee of two separate trusts is in default in one of the trusts and is a beneficiary in the other trust, then his beneficial interest in the second trust cannot be impounded to make good his default in the first trust.[13]

What if a beneficiary requests the trustee to commit a breach of trust, and he complies? This case is governed by section 62 of the Trustee Act, 1925, which, as amended by the Married Women (Restraint upon Anticipation) Act, 1949, provides that:

> Where a trustee commits a breach of trust at the instigation or request or with the consent in writing of a beneficiary, the court may, if it thinks fit, make such order as to the court seems just, for impounding all or any part of the interest of the beneficiary in the trust estate by way of indemnity to the trustee or persons claiming through him.

The right of a trustee, who has committed a breach of trust at the instigation of a beneficiary, to impound the beneficiary's interest under this section, does not entitle the trustee to insist on remaining a trustee until he has exercised this right. The right of the trustee to impound is not

---

[11] *In re Dacre*, [1916] 1 Ch. 344.
[12] *Doering* v. *Doering* (1889) 42 Ch. D. 203.
[13] *In re Towndrow*, [1911] 1 Ch. 662.

limited to the case where the trustee was an existing trustee, but could be exercised also by a former trustee.[14]

It will be observed that what can be impounded under the section is 'the interest of the beneficiary in the trust estate'.

So if a son, on his marriage, assigns his reversionary interest under his parents' marriage settlement to trustees of his own marriage settlement, who gave notice of their interest, then if the son instigates the trustees of the first settlement to commit a breach of trust by applying capital in discharging his debts, there is no 'interest of the beneficiary in the trust estate' that can be impounded to indemnify the trustees of the first settlement, since by the assignment the son had divested himself of his beneficial interest under the first settlement.[15]

(E) STATUTORY PROTECTION

(1) TRUSTEE ACT, 1925

Section 61 of this Act reads as follows:

If it appears to the court that a trustee, whether appointed by the court or otherwise, is or may be personally liable for any breach of trust, whether the transaction alleged to be a breach of trust occurred before or after the commencement of this Act, but has acted honestly and reasonably, and ought fairly to be excused for the breach of trust and for omitting to obtain the directions of the court in the matter in which he committed such breach, then the court may relieve him either wholly or partly from personal liability for the same.

This section re-enacted section 3 of the Judicial Trustee Act, 1896, and the following observations on that section were made by Byrne, J., in *In re Turner*:[16]

'I think that the section relied on is meant to be acted upon freely and fairly in the exercise of judicial discretion, but I think the court ought to be satisfied, before exercising the very large powers conferred upon it, by sufficient evidence, that the trustee acted reasonably. I do not think that I have sufficient evidence in this case that he so acted; in fact, it does not appear from the letters that Mr. Turner acted in respect of this mortgage as he would probably have acted had it been a transaction of his own. I think that if he was—and he well may have been—a businesslike man, he would not, before lending his money, have been satisfied without some further inquiry as to the means of the mortgagor and as to the nature and value of the property upon which he was about to advance his money.'

The fact that a trustee is remunerated does not disentitle him from relief under the section, but the fact that he is remunerated is a circumstance

[14] *In re Pauling's Settlement Trusts (No. 2)*, [1963] 2 W.L.R. 839.
[15] *Ricketts* v. *Ricketts*, [1891] 64 L.T. 263.
[16] [1897] 1 Ch. 536, 542.

52 AN OUTLINE OF THE LAW OF TRUSTS

taken into consideration by the Court when exercising its discretion.[17] So where a banker undertook to act as a paid trustee of a settlement created by a customer and so deliberately placed himself in a position where his duty as trustee conflicted with his interest as a banker, the Court should be slow to relieve him under section 61.[18]

(2) STATUTE OF LIMITATION, 1939

Before a beneficiary takes action against a trustee for breach of trust there are two matters he must consider.

Firstly the equitable doctrine of 'laches', which rules that if there has been undue delay in taking action against the trustee, then the beneficiary will be deemed to have waived his right.

Secondly, are there any time limits in the Statute of Limitations Act, 1939, affecting his right?

The relevant provisions can be considered under three headings.

(a) Generally

Section 19 (2) of the Act provides that a claim by a beneficiary in respect of any breach of trust for which no period of limitation is prescribed by the Act shall be barred after six years.

(b) Other periods of limitation

Two cases may be noted in which a period of twelve years is prescribed by the Act.

(i) An action for the recovery of land (s.4(3)).
(ii) An action in respect of a claim for the personal estate of a deceased person, testate or intestate (s.20).

(c) No period of limitation prescribed

Section 19 (2) provides that no period of limitation prescribed by the Act shall apply to an action by a beneficiary, being an action:

(i) in respect of any fraud or fraudulent breach of trust to which the trustee was a party or privy; or
(ii) to recover from the trustee trust property, or the proceeds thereof, in his possession, or previously received by the trustee and converted to his use.

[17] *National Trustees Co.* v. *General Finance Co.*, [1905] A.C. 373.
[18] *In re Pauling's Settlement Trusts*, [1963] 3 W.L.R. 742.

But even in these two cases the beneficiary may lose his right of action by 'laches' since section 29 of the Act provides that 'nothing in the Act shall affect any equitable jurisdiction to refuse relief on the ground of acquiescence or otherwise'.

The right of action accrues generally when the breach is committed, but where a beneficiary is entitled to a future interest in the trust property, his right of action is not deemed to arise until the interest falls into possession.[19] This, however, does not prevent a remainderman taking action during the prior interest of a life tenant.

As a general example, if during the life tenancy of A, the trustees make unauthorised advances of capital to B, and A either takes no action or is barred from taking action, then if X, one of the remaindermen, before his interest falls into possession takes action resulting in the trustees having to replace the capital, such action by X will not benefit A and the trustees will be entitled to the income on the capital replaced to the exclusion of A, the life tenant.[20] This follows from section 19(3) of the Act which provides:

No beneficiary as against whom there would be a good defence under this Act shall derive any greater or other benefit from a judgment or order obtained by any other beneficiary than he could have obtained if he had brought the action and this Act had been pleaded in defence.

Finally it may be mentioned that the trust instrument may exonerate the trustee from liability except in the case of wilful default.[21]

[19] Proviso to section 19(2).
[20] *In re Somerset*, [1894] 1 Ch .231.
[21] For meaning of wilful default, *see* p. 49, *supra*.

8 Appointment, Retirement and Removal of Trustees

IN express trusts, the instrument creating the trust names the first trustees, but any one so appointed is perfectly free to disclaim. Where individuals, as opposed to a trust corporation, are appointed, death or incapacity will or may create vacancies, which will require filling.

Section 36 of the Trustee Act, 1925, reads:

(1) Where a trustee, either original or substituted, and whether appointed by a court or otherwise, is dead, or remains out of the United Kingdom for more than twelve months, or desires to be discharged from all or any of the trusts or powers reposed in or conferred on him, or refuses or is unfit to act therein, or is incapable of acting therein, or is an infant, then, subject to the restrictions imposed by this Act on the number[1] of trustees,—

    (a) the person or persons nominated for the purpose of appointing new trustees by the instrument, if any, creating the trust; or

    (b) if there is no such person, or no such person able and willing to act, then the surviving or continuing trustees or trustee for the time being, or the personal representatives of the last surviving or continuing trustee;

may, by writing, appoint one or more other persons (whether or not being the persons exercising the power) to be a trustee or trustees in the place of the trustee so deceased remaining out of the United Kingdom, desiring to be discharged, refusing, or being unfit or being incapable, or being an infant, as aforesaid.

If the settlor has nominated the person or persons to appoint new trustees, then section 36(1) (a) above will apply. Occasionally instead of giving his nominee a general power, the settlor limits the nomination to certain specified events. If the event creating the vacancy is not one contemplated by the power, then the nominee is not within section 36(1) (a) and hence the proper person to appoint the new trustee must be found in section 36(1) (b).[2]

Where a trustee wishes to retire, and the vacancy thereby created is

---

[1] For the statutory provisions regarding the number of trustees, *see* p. 11, *ante.*
[2] *In re Wheeler*, [1896] 1 Ch. 315.

filled, the retirement and new appointment are effected under section 36(1), Trustee Act, 1925.

Where there is a retirement without a new appointment, the retirement is effected under section 39, Trustee Act, 1925, as follows:

39. (1) Where a trustee is desirous of being discharged from the trust, and after his discharge there will be either a trust corporation or at least two individuals to act as trustees to perform the trust, then, if such trustee as aforesaid by deed declares that he is desirous of being discharged from the trust, and if his co-trustees and such other person, if any, as is empowered to appoint trustees, by deed consent to the discharge of the trustee, and to the vesting in the co-trustees alone of the trust property, the trustee desirous of being discharged shall be deemed to have retired from the trust, and shall, by the deed, be discharged therefrom under this Act, without any new trustee being appointed in his place.

(2) Any assurance or thing requisite for vesting the trust property in the continuing trustees alone shall be executed or done.

Independently of statute, a trustee may retire:

(a) under provision made to that end in the trust instrument, or
(b) where all the beneficiaries are *sui juris* and they consent to the trustee retiring.

If the circumstances are such that an appointment cannot be made under section 36(1), *supra*, then an application can be made to the Court under section 41(1). This reads:

41. (1) The court may, whenever it is expedient to appoint a new trustee or new trustees, and it is found inexpedient difficult or impracticable so to do without the assistance of the court, make an order appointing a new trustee or new trustees either in substitution for or in addition to any existing trustee or trustees, or although there is no existing trustee.

In particular and without prejudice to the generality of the foregoing provision, the court may make an order appointing a new trustee in substitution for a trustee who is convicted of felony, or is a lunatic or a defective, or is a bankrupt, or is a corporation which is in liquidation or has been dissolved.

However, applications should not be made to the Court where the power of appointing new trustees contained in section 36(1), Trustee Act, 1925, can be exercised.[3]

Very occasionally a trustee acts in a manner that is against the best interests of the trust. In such case an application may be made to the Court, which has jurisdiction, apart from statute, to remove a trustee.

In order for the application to be successful 'you must find something which induces the court to think either that the trust property will not be safe, or that the trust will not be properly executed in the interests of the beneficiaries'.[4]

---

[3] *In re Gibbon's Trust* (1882) 45 L.T. 756.
[4] *Per* Warrington, J., in *In re Wrightson*, [1908] 1 Ch. 789, 803.

9 Miscellaneous Matters

(A) SPECIAL RIGHTS OF BENEFICIARIES

(1) PUTTING AN END TO THE TRUST

Equity does not want a trustee and if the beneficiary is *sui juris* and his interest is an absolute indefeasible one, he can call on the trustee to transfer the trust property to him, since a trustee is perfectly safe in taking a receipt and discharge from such a beneficiary.[1]

If there are several beneficiaries, who are all *sui juris* and absolutely entitled to the property, they may call for a distribution amongst them, if they act in concert.

(2) FOLLOWING THE TRUST PROPERTY

In Chapter 7 it was explained that beneficiaries in the case of breach of trust could take action against the trustee, but there is an added right open to them and that is to follow the property.

Whether a sale by a trustee is rightful or wrongful, the beneficiary can elect to take the sale proceeds, if he can identify them.[2] The court attributes the ownership of the trust property to the *cestui que trust* so long as it can be traced.[3] But actual identification is not possible in many cases and equity has modified the view expressed in the *Hallett's Estate* case as to identification and now 'it found no difficulty in regarding a composite fund as an amalgam constituted by the mixture of two or more funds, each of which could be regarded as having for certain purposes, a continued separate existence. Putting it another way, equity regarded the amalgam as capable in proper circumstances, of being resolved into its component parts'.[4]

The manner in which the trace is effected will now be considered under a number of headings.

(*a*) The trustee has used the proceeds in a purchase of land or securities.
    In this case the beneficiary has a right of election either to take the

---

[1] *Saunders* v. *Vautier* (1841) 4 Beav. 115.
[2] *In re Hallett's Estate* (1880) 13 Ch. D. 696.
[3] *Per* Wood, V-C., in *Frith* v. *Cartland* (1865) 2 H. & M. 417, 421.
[4] *In re Diplock*, [1948] Ch. 465, 520.

property or to take a charge on the property for the amount of the sale proceeds.[5]

(b) The trustee has mixed trust assets with his own in such a way that they could not be sufficiently distinguished and treated separately. In this case the onus is on him to distinguish the separate assets, and to the extent that he fails to do so they belong to the trust.[6]

(c) The trustee has mixed the trust money with his own in making the purchase.

Here the beneficiary could claim a charge on the property for the amount of the trust moneys expended in the purchase. Furthermore, the beneficiary could elect either to treat the property as trust property or to treat it as security for the recoupment of the trust moneys; and the right of election also applied where the property was purchased by the trustee in part out of his own moneys and in part out of the trust moneys, so that the beneficiary might, if he wished, require the property to be treated as trust property with regard to the proportion of it which the trust moneys contributed.[7]

(d) The trustee has mixed the funds of two or more trusts. Here the beneficiary of one fund is not in conscience bound to give precedence to the beneficiary of the other fund, so if there is a deficiency the two beneficiaries must share the loss *pari passu*.[8]

(e) The trustee has paid the proceeds into his own bank, so they are mixed with his own moneys.

(i) The rule in *Clayton's* case[9] does not apply if there is only one trust involved. Consequently withdrawals from the accounts are set against the trustee's own money until it is exhausted.[10]

(ii) If there are two or more trusts involved, then as between beneficiaries of the same trustee under different trusts, the rule in *Clayton's* case does apply for the very good reason there is no other practical solution.[11]

There can be no following property where the trustee has dissipated the proceeds entirely.

It remains to consider the case where trust property has passed, maybe

[5] *In re Hallett's Estate, supra.*
[6] *Lupton* v. *White* (1808) 15 Ves. 432.
[7] *In re Tilley's Will Trusts*, [1967] 2 W.L.R. 1533.
[8] *In re Diplock, supra.*
[9] This rule raises a presumption in the case of an unbroken current account that the first in is first out (FIFO).
[10] *In re Hallett's Estate, supra.*
[11] *Hancock* v. *Smith* (1889) 41 Ch. D. 456; *In re Stenning*, [1895] 2 Ch. 433.

as a gift, from the trustee to a volunteer (i.e. one who has not given valuable consideration for the property) who takes without notice.[12]

Here the equities are equal since both the beneficiary and the volunteer are innocent. No difficulty arises if, for example, the volunteer placed the trust money on deposit with a bank. The claim of the beneficiary under the trust is paramount. On the other hand, if the volunteer has mixed the trust money with his own, then both being innocent, if there has to be an abatement, they rank *pari passu*.[13]

Finally, if the innocent volunteer has expended the trust money that has come into his hands in making alterations to his residence, there can be no tracing since this remedy could only be effected by giving the beneficiary a charge on the volunteer's residence, enforceable by sale, which would be quite inequitable.[14]

(3) RIGHT TO ACCOUNTS AND PRODUCTION OF DOCUMENTS

The duty of trustees to keep accounts has been touched on in Chapter 6 and it now remains to consider the beneficiary's right to copies of the accounts and production of trust documents.

The right to copies of the trustees' accounts would extend to production of vouchers supporting the accounts. In addition a beneficiary is entitled to inspect title deeds and documents,[15] subject to this limitation, that trustees cannot be called upon to produce documents, e.g. minutes of their proceedings, showing how they have exercised their discretion, or giving reasons for their decisions, for if such matters are not protected from disclosure, trustees could not perform their duties efficiently.[16]

(B) VARIATION OF THE TERMS OF THE TRUST

When all the beneficiaries are *sui juris*, they can all agree to any variation of the terms of the trust, just as under the rule in *Saunders* v. *Vautier* they can put an end to the trust.

Here we are concerned with cases where there are infant and possibly unborn beneficiaries and application must be made to the court for approval of any proposed variation if such beneficiaries are to be bound. The problem must be considered under two headings.

---

[12] Here it should be mentioned that there can be no following trust property into the hands of a bona fide purchaser for value without notice.
[13] *In re Diplock, supra.*
[14] ibid.
[15] *In re Cowin* (1886) 33 Ch. D. 179.
[16] *In re Marquess of Londonderry's Settlement*, [1964] Ch. 594.

(1) VARIATIONS FOR ADMINISTRATIVE PURPOSES

(*a*) On grounds of expediency under section 57, Trustee Act, 1925, which
provides:

'Where in the management or administration of any property vested in trustees,
any sale, lease, mortgage, surrender, release or other disposition or any purchase, investment, acquisition, expenditure, or other transaction is in the
opinion of the court expedient, but the same cannot be effected by reason of
the absence of any power for that purpose vested in the trustees by the trust
instrument, if any, or by law, the court may by order confer upon the trustees,
either generally or in any particular instance, the necessary power for the
purpose, on such terms, and subject to such provisions and conditions, if any,
as the court may think fit and may direct in what manner any money authorised
to be expended, and the costs of any transaction, are to be paid or borne as
between capital and income.'

The object of this section 'was to secure that trust property should be
managed as advantageously as possible in the interests of the beneficiaries,
and with that object in view, to authorise specific dealings with the property
which the court might have felt itself unable to sanction under the inherent
jurisdiction, either because there was no actual emergency or because of
inability to show that the position which called for intervention was one
which the creator of the trust could not reasonably have foreseen; but it
was no part of the legislative aim to disturb the rule that the court will not
rewrite a trust.'[17] So the Court cannot under section 57 alter the beneficial
interests.

(*b*) Section 15, Trustee Investments Act, 1961.
This section provides:

'The enlargement of the investment powers of trustees by this Act shall not
lessen any power of a court to confer wider powers of investment on trustees,
or affect the extent to which any such power is to be exercised'.

But the Courts have declined to extend investment powers beyond
those conferred by this Act save in exceptional circumstances.[18]

(*c*) Section 53, Trustee Act, 1925.
This section provides:

'Where an infant is beneficially entitled to any property the court may, with a
view to the application of the capital or income thereof for the maintenance,
education, or benefit of the infant, make an order—

    (a) appointing a person to convey such property; or
    (b) in the case of stock, or a thing in action, vesting in any person the right

[17] *In re Downshire's Settled Estates*, [1953] 218, 248.
[18] *In re Kolb's Will Trusts*, [1962] Ch. 531.

to transfer or call for a transfer of such stock, or to receive the dividends or income thereof, or to sue for and recover such thing in action, upon such terms as the court may think fit.'

In addition to these statutory provisions, the Court has inherent jurisdiction to authorise otherwise unauthorised acts of management or administration of the trust property in cases of:

(a) Emergency, i.e. one not foreseen or anticipated by the creator of the trust, and which must be dealt with at once.
(b) Salvage.
   In this case the court can authorise the expenditure of capital money in doing repairs which are absolutely necessary for the preservation of the property.[19]

Where the rights of the beneficiaries under a trust are the subject of doubt or dispute, the Court has for long had an inherent jurisdiction to approve on behalf of all interested parties, whether adult, infant or unborn, compromises of such disputes.[20] What it will not do is to authorise a variation, agreed between the parties, of a trust instrument under the guise of a compromise of a dispute.[21]

(2) VARIATION OF TRUSTS ACT, 1958

In *Chapman* v. *Chapman*[22] the House of Lords held that the Court had no inherent jurisdiction to approve the variation of trusts on behalf of infant or unborn persons. This decision led to the Variation of Trusts Act, 1958, the provisions of which will be dealt with briefly.

Section 1 of the Act provides:

Where property, whether real or personal, is held on trusts arising, whether before or after the passing of this Act, under any will, settlement or other disposition, the court may if it thinks fit by order approve on behalf of—

(a) any person having, directly or indirectly, an interest, whether vested or contingent, under the trusts who by reason of infancy or other incapacity is incapable of assenting, or
(b) any person (whether ascertained or not) who may become entitled, directly or indirectly, to an interest under the trusts as being at a future date or on the happening of a future event a person of any specified description or a member of any specified class of persons, so however

---

[19] *In re Willis*, [1902] 1 Ch. 15.
[20] *In re Trenchard*, [1902] 2 Ch. 378.
[21] *In re Powell-Cotton's Resettlement*, [1956] 1 W.L.R. 23.
[22] [1954] A.C. 299.

that this paragraph shall not include any person who would be of that description, or a member of that class, as the case may be, if the said date had fallen or the said event had happened at the date of the application to the court, or

(c) any person unborn, or

(d) any person in respect of any discretionary interest of his under protective trusts where the interest of the principal beneficiary has not failed or determined,

any arrangement (by whomsoever proposed, and whether or not there is any other person beneficially interested who is capable of assenting thereto) varying or revoking all or any of the trusts, or enlarging the powers of the trustees of managing or administering any of the property subject to the trusts:

Provided that except by virtue of paragraph (d) of this subsection the court shall not approve an arrangement on behalf of any person unless the carrying out thereof would be for the benefit of that person.

To understand the purpose behind the Act of 1958, it is necessary to go back to *Chapman* v. *Chapman*,[23] a case in which the Court was asked to approve variations of the terms of a trust with the avowed object of mini-mising the prospective liability to estate duty. Many settlements confer successive life interests, resulting in a liability to estate duty on the capital of the trust on the death of a life tenant. The rate of charge in many cases is increased by aggregation. If equitable arrangements could be made for dividing the capital between the life tenants and remainderman there could be a considerable saving if the life tenant survived for a period of five years, and a reduced saving if surviving two years. Should the remain-derman be an infant, then the arrangement could not be effected unless the Court could be persuaded to approve the scheme as a 'compromise'. As stated above, the House of Lords decided that the Court had no power to give its consent to such proposals, and Lord Morton of Henryton stated that if the court had power to approve and did approve schemes for avoiding taxation 'the way would open for a most undignified game of chess between the Chancery Division and the legislature'.

In spite of these observations, many schemes, having for their object the saving of taxation, have been approved by the Court under the Variation of Trusts Act, 1958. In a recent case,[24] where the motive of the scheme of arrangement to vary the trusts of a settlement was to put certain bene-ficiaries in a better position so far as capital gains tax was concerned, Goff, J., decided that it was a perfectly legitimate motive for seeking the Court's sanction of the arrangement, and so long as he was satisfied that the scheme was for the benefit of infants and unborn persons, it was his duty to sanction it.

---

[23] *supra.*
[24] *In re Sainsbury's Settlement*, [1967] 1 W.L.R. 476.

Coming back to section 1 of the 1958 Act, it will be noticed that there are four classes of beneficiaries, on whose behalf the Court can approve variation of the terms of a trust.

Class (*a*) covers infants and other persons who by reason of incapacity (e.g. lunacy) are incapable of assenting to the scheme.

Class (*b*) covers persons (ascertained or not) having contingent interests in the trust fund. The future spouse of a specified person would be included by reason of the words in brackets.[25]

Class (*c*) covers unborn persons.

Class (*d*) covers a beneficiary who has or may have a discretionary interest under a protective trust.

Before the Court can approve a scheme of arrangement on behalf of any person who is in or may become within one of the first three classes, it must be satisfied that the arrangement is for the benefit of that person.[26] The benefit need not come out of the trust fund, but may arise from an independent source, such as the personal covenant of a financially responsible individual.[27]

Exceptionally, the Court when approving a scheme of arrangement under the Act, does not have to be satisfied that it is for the benefit of a beneficiary in the fourth class.[26]

Although the consent of the trustees is not required under the Act, the Court pays great attention to their views and in practice it would not sanction an arrangement if the trustees show good reasons for their opposition.[28]

[25] *See In re Clitheroe's Settlement Trusts*, [1959] 1 W.L.R. 1159.
[26] Proviso to section 1. Variation of Trusts Act, 1958.
[27] *In re Clitheroe's Settlement Trusts, supra.*
[28] *In re Steed's Will Trusts*, [1960] Ch. 407.

Perpetuities and Accumulations

RULE AGAINST PERPETUITIES

FROM the earliest times the Courts have set their face against the tying up of property in such a way as to render the estate in such property inalienable. 'It is the policy of the law to make estates alienable.'[1]

Suppose for example a bequest was made to any grandchild of A, a bachelor, who shall pass the final examination of the Institute of Chartered Accountants. Such a bequest is riddled with contingencies to such an extent that the personal representative would have great difficulty in determining the beneficiary.

To guard against such remoteness of vesting, the law has invented the *Rule against Perpetuities*, which is 'strict and highly technical in its operation',[2] in spite of the statutory policy to remove the harshness of the rule.

Before setting out the rule, it is necessary to be quite clear as to the distinction between vested and contingent interests.

'An estate is vested, when there is an immediate fixed right of present or future enjoyment. An estate is vested in possession, when there exists a right of present enjoyment. An estate is vested in interest when there is a present fixed right of future enjoyment. An estate is contingent when a right of enjoyment is to accrue, on an event which is dubious and uncertain.'[3]

Examples:

A dies, bequeathing to B, an adult, his residuary estate. On A's death B has an estate vested in possession in the residue.

C dies, bequeathing to D, an infant, his residuary estate when he attains twenty-one. On C's death, B has an estate vested in interest in the residue.

E dies, bequeathing to F, his residuary estate if he attains twenty-one. On E's death, F's estate in the residue is contingent on his attaining twenty-one years of age.

[1] *Per* Fry, L.J., in *In re Parry and Daggs* (1885) 31 Ch. D. 130, 134.
[2] *Per* Greene, M.R., in *In re Legh's Settlement*, [1938] Ch. 39, 44.
[3] *Fearne on Contingent Remainders*, 10th ed. (1844).

The full meaning of 'vested' has been given, because of its importance in the law of trusts, but for purpose of the perpetuities rule, a gift becomes vested when it ceases to be contingent.

In the first place the rule as it existed before the coming into operation of the Perpetuities and Accumulations Act, 1964,[4] will be set out. The rule is stated in *Lewin on Trusts*[5] thus:

'A future equitable interest will be void if it may by possibility vest outside the perpetuity period, that is the period of a life or any number of lives in being at the creation of the trust plus twenty one years plus any period of gestation'.

In the case of an *inter-vivos* settlement the creation of the trust is the date of the settlement; in the case of a testamentary trust it is the death of the testator. Section 1 of the 1964 Act empowers the creator of the trust to specify a period not exceeding eighty years instead of the usual twenty-one.[6]

Unless at the time of the creation of the trust it is possible to postulate with certainty that the future interest will vest within the perpetuity period, it is void. Apart from section 3 of the 1964 Act, it is not permissible to 'wait and see'. If it could vest either inside or outside the period then section 3 permits the principle of 'wait and see' to apply.

The lives in being must be human beings alive or *en ventre sa mère* at the time the trust is created, and may be mentioned specifically or by inference.

Prior to the 1964 Act, a man or woman, however old, was always deemed capable of having children. So if a testator, who was survived by his parents, made a bequest to the children of his brothers and sisters, it would be void under the rule, on the grounds that further children might be born to the testator's parents, though they were both sixty-six years of age.[7]

Under section 2(1) (*a*) of the 1964 Act there is a presumption that a male can have a child at the age of fourteen or over and that a female can have a child at the age of twelve or over but not if she is over the age of fifty-five.

In relation to class gifts the rule is 'that the limitation must be such that every member of the class . . . must of necessity take within the time allowed',[8] but under section 4 of the 1964 Act a gift to a class as a whole is saved by eliminating potential or unborn members whose inclusion would have rendered the gift void for remoteness.

By section 163, Law of Property Act, 1925, where under instruments coming into operation after 1925, gifts would be void as offending against

---

[4] This act came into force on 16 July 1964 and will be referred to as the 1964 Act.
[5] 16th ed., p. 71.
[6] As to a disposition under a special power of appointment, *see* section 3(2) of the 1964 Act.
[7] *Ward* v. *Van der Loeff*, [1924] A.C. 653.
[8] *Per* Chitty, J., in *In re Dawson* (1888) 39 Ch. D. 155, 164.

the rule because the vesting was to depend on the attainment by the beneficiary, or the members of a class of beneficiaries, of an age exceeding twenty-one years, then the instrument was to take effect as if the age of twenty-one substituted for the age stated in the instrument.

This section was repealed by the 1964 Act, and section 4(1) of that Act provides that where a disposition is limited by reference to the attainment by any person or persons of a specified age exceeding twenty-one years, and it is apparent at the time the disposition is made or becomes apparent at a subsequent time—

(a) that the disposition would, apart from this section, be void for remoteness, but

(b) that it would not be so void if the specified age had been twenty-one,

the disposition shall be treated for all purposes as if, instead of being limited by reference to the age in fact specified, it had been limited by reference to the age nearest to that age which would, if specified instead, have prevented the disposition from being so void.

TRUSTS FOR ACCUMULATION

Any direction in a trust instrument to accumulate the income of property for a period longer than—

(a) the life of the settlor; or

(b) twenty-one years from the death of the settlor; or

(c) the minority or respective minorities of any person or persons living or *en ventre sa mère* at the death of the settlor; or

(d) the minority or respective minorities only of any person or persons who under the trusts of the settlement would, for the time being, if of full age, be entitled to the income directed to be accumulated, is void as soon as the relevant authorised period is exceeded.[9]

In the case of instruments coming into force after 15 July 1964, section 13 of the Act of 1964 prescribes two further periods for which accumulations of income may be permitted, namely:

(a) a term of twenty-one years from the date of the making the disposition,[10] and

(b) the duration of the minority or respective minorities of any person or persons in being at that date.

[9] Law of Property Act, 1925, s.164.
[10] 'Disposition' includes the conferring of a power of appointment and any other disposition of an interest in or right over property, section 13 of the 1964 Act.

The restrictions on accumulations that have been noted do not extend to any provision:

(*a*) for the payment of the debts of the settlor or any other person,
(*b*) for the raising of portions for

    (i) children of the settlor, or
    (ii) children of any person taking an interest under the settlement.

The two subjects discussed in this Appendix are, as has been mentioned, highly technical and if more detailed information is required, reference should be made to one of the standard works on trusts.

Trustee Investments Act, 1961

9 & 10 Eliz. 2 Ch. **62**

ARRANGEMENT OF SECTIONS

1. New powers of investment of trustees.
2. Restrictions on wider-range investment.
3. Relationship between Act and other powers of investment.
4. Interpretation of references to trust property and trust funds.
5. Certain valuations to be conclusive for purposes of divison of trust fund.
6. Duty of trustees in choosing investments.
7. Application of ss.1–6 to persons, other than trustees, having trustee investment powers.
8. Application of ss.1–6 in special cases.
9. Supplementary provisions as to investments.
10. Powers of Scottish trustees supplementary to powers of investment.
11. Local Authority investment schemes.
12. Power to confer additional powers of investment.
13. Power to modify provisions as to division of trust fund.
14. Amendment of s.27 of Trusts (Scotland) Act, 1921.
15. Saving for powers of court.
16. Minor and consequential amendments and repeals.
17. Short title, extent and construction.

SCHEDULES:

First Schedule—Manner of Investment.
Second Schedule—Modification of s.2 in relation to property falling within s.3 (3).
Third Schedule—Provisions supplementary to s.3 (4).
Fourth Schedule—Minor and consequential amendments.
Fifth Schedule—Repeals.

AMENDMENTS MADE BY STATUTORY INSTRUMENTS SINCE
3 AUGUST 1961

FIRST SCHEDULE

Part I: Narrower-Range Investments not requiring advice

Additions to para. 1:

Ulster Development Bonds[1]

National Development Bonds[2]

Fixed-interest securities issued in

U.K. by Inter-American Bank[3]

British Savings Bonds[6]

Part II: Narrower-Range Investments requiring advice
Additions to:

Para. 7. Bank of Ireland 7% Loan Stock 1986/91[4]

Para 9 (f). The Great Ouse Water Authority[5]

An Act to make fresh provision with respect to investment by trustees and persons having the investment powers of trustees, and by local authorities, and for purposes connected therewith. [3rd August, 1961]

NEW POWERS OF INVESTMENT OF TRUSTEES

1.—(1) A trustee may invest any property in his hands, whether at the time in a state of investment or not, in any manner specified in Part I or II of the First Schedule to this Act or, subject to the next following section, in any manner specified in Part III of that Schedule, and may also from time to time vary any such investments.

(2) The supplemental provisions contained in Part IV of that Schedule shall have effect for the interpretation and for restricting the operation of the said Parts I to III.

(3) No provision relating to the powers of the trustee contained in any instrument (not being an enactment or an instrument made under an enactment) made before the passing of this Act shall limit the powers conferred by this section, but those powers are exerciseable only in so far

[1] Trustee Investments (Additional Powers) (No. 2) Order, 1962, (S.I. 1962, No. 2611).
[2] Trustee Investments (Additional Powers) Order, 1964 (S.I. 1964, No. 703).
[3] Trustee Investments (Additional Powers) (No. 2) Order, 1964 (S.I. 1964, No. 1404).
[4] Trustee Investments (Additional Powers) Order, 1966 (S.I. 1966, No. 401).
[5] Trustee Investments (Additional Powers) Order, 1962 (S.I. 1962, No. 658).
[6] Trustee Investments (Additional Powers) Order, 1968 (S.I. 1868, No. 470).

as a contrary intention is not expressed in any Act or instrument made under an enactment, whenever passed or made, and so relating or in any other instrument so relating which is made after the passing of this Act.

For the purposes of this subsection any rule of the law of Scotland whereby a testamentary writing may be deemed to be made on a date other than that on which it was actually executed shall be disregarded.

(4) In this Act "narrower-range investment" means an investment falling within Part I or II of the First Schedule to this Act and "wider-range investment" means an investment falling within Part III of that Schedule.

RESTRICTIONS ON WIDER-RANGE INVESTMENT

2.—(1) A trustee shall not have power by virtue of the foregoing section to make or retain any wider-range investment unless the trust fund has been divided into two parts (hereinafter referred to as the narrower-range part and the wider-range part), the parts being, subject to the provisions of this Act, equal in value at the time of the division; and where such a division has been made no subsequent division of the same fund shall be made for the purposes of this section, and no property shall be transferred from one part of the fund to the other unless either—

(a) the transfer is authorised or required by the following provisions of this Act, or

(b) a compensating transfer is made at the same time.

In this section "compensating transfer", in relation to any transferred property, means a transfer in the opposite direction of property of equal value.

(2) Property belonging to the narrower-range part of a trust fund shall not by virtue of the foregoing section be invested except in narrower-range investments, and any property invested in any other manner which is or becomes comprised in that part of the trust fund shall either be transferred to the wider-range part of the fund, with a compensating transfer, or be reinvested in narrower-range investments as soon as may be.

(3) Where any property accrues to a trust fund after the fund has been divided in pursuance of subsection (1) of this section, then—

(a) if the property accrues to the trustee as owner or former owner of property comprised in either part of the fund, it shall be treated as belonging to that part of the fund;

(b) in any other case, the trustee shall secure, by apportionment of the accruing property or the transfer of property from one part of the fund to the other, or both, that the value of each part of the fund is increased by the same amount.

Where a trustee acquires property in consideration of a money payment the acquisition of the property shall be treated for the purposes of this section as investment and not as the accrual of property to the trust fund notwithstanding that the amount of the consideration is less than the value of the property acquired; and paragraph (a) of this subsection shall not include the case of a dividend or interest becoming part of a trust fund

(4) Where in the exercise of any power or duty of a trustee property falls to be taken out of the trust fund, nothing in this section shall restrict his discretion as to the choice of property to be taken out.

RELATIONSHIP BETWEEN ACT AND OTHER POWERS OF INVESTMENT

3.—(1) The powers conferred by section one of this Act are in addition to and not in derogation from any power conferred otherwise than by this Act of investment or postponing conversion exerciseable by a trustee (hereinafter referred to as a "special power").

(2) Any special power (however expressed) to invest property in any investment for the time being authorised by law for the investment of trust property, being a power conferred on a trustee before the passing of this Act or conferred on him under any enactment passed before the passing of this Act, shall have effect as a power to invest property in like manner and subject to the like provisions as under the foregoing provisions of this Act

(3) In relation to property, including wider-range but not including narrower-range investments,—

(a) which a trustee is authorised to hold apart from—

  (i) the provisions of section one of this Act or any of the provisions of Part I of the Trustee Act, 1925, or any of the provisions of the Trusts (Scotland) Act, 1921, or

  (ii) any such power to invest in authorised investments as is mentioned in the foregoing subsection, or

(b) which became part of a trust fund in consequence of the exercise by the trustee, as owner of property falling within this subsection, of any power conferred by subsection (3) or (4) of section ten of the Trustee Act, 1925, or paragraph (o) or (p) of subsection (1) of section four of the Trusts (Scotland) Act, 1921,

the foregoing section shall have effect subject to the modifications set out in the Second Schedule to this Act.

(4) The foregoing subsection shall not apply where the powers of the

trustee to invest or postpone conversion have been conferred or varied—

(a) by an order of any court made within the period of ten years ending with the passing of this Act, or

(b) by any enactment passed, or instrument having effect under an enactment made, within that period, being an enactment or instrument relating specifically to the trusts in question; or

(c) by an enactment contained in a local Act of the present Session;

but the provisions of the Third Schedule to this Act shall have effect in a case falling within this subsection.

INTERPRETATION OF REFERENCES TO TRUST PROPERTY AND TRUST FUNDS

4.—(1) In this Act "property" includes real or personal property of any description, including money and things in action:

Provided that it does not include an interest in expectancy, but the falling into possession of such an interest, or the receipt of proceeds of the sale thereof, shall be treated for the purposes of this Act as an accrual of property to the trust fund.

(2) So much of the property in the hands of a trustee shall for the purposes of this Act constitute one trust fund as is held on trusts which (as respects the beneficiaries or their respective interests or the purposes of the trust or as respects the powers of the trustee) are not identical with those on which any other property in his hands is held.

(3) Where property is taken out of a trust fund by way of appropriation so as to form a separate fund, and at the time of the appropriation the trust fund had (as to the whole or a part thereof) been divided in pursuance of subsection (1) of section two of this Act, or that subsection as modified by the Second Schedule to this Act, then if the separate fund is so divided the narrower-range and wider-range parts of the separate fund may be constituted so as either to be equal, or to bear to each other the same proportion as the two corresponding parts of the fund out of which it was so appropriated (the values of those parts of those funds being ascertained as at the time of appropriation), or some intermediate proportion.

(4) In the application of this section to Scotland the following subsection shall be substituted for subsection (1) thereof:—

"(1) In this Act 'property' includes property of any description (whether heritable or moveable, corporeal or incorporeal) which is presently enjoyable, but does not include a future interest, whether vested or contingent."

CERTAIN VALUATIONS TO BE CONCLUSIVE FOR PURPOSES OF
DIVISION OF TRUST FUND

5.—(1) If for the purposes of section two or four of this Act or the Second Schedule thereto a trustee obtains, from a person reasonably believed by the trustee to be qualified to make it, a valuation in writing of any property, the valuation shall be conclusive in determining whether the division of the trust fund in pursuance of subsection (1) of the said section two, or any transfer or apportionment of property under that section or the said Second Schedule, has been duly made.

(2) The foregoing subsection applies to any such valuation notwithstanding that it is made by a person in the course of his employment as an officer or servant.

DUTY OF TRUSTEES IN CHOOSING INVESTMENTS

6.—(1) In the exercise of his powers of investment a trustee shall have regard—

(a) to the need for diversification of investments of the trust in so far as is appropriate to the circumstances of the trust;

(b) to the suitability to the trust of investments of the description of investment proposed and of the investment proposed as an investment of that description.

(2) Before exercising any power conferred by section one of this Act to invest in a manner specified in Part II or III of the First Schedule to this Act, or before investing in any such manner in the exercise of a power falling within subsection (2) of section three of this Act, a trustee shall obtain and consider proper advice on the question whether the investment is satisfactory having regard to the matters mentioned in paragraphs (a) and (b) of the foregoing subsection.

(3) A trustee retaining any investment made in the exercise of such a power and in such a manner as aforesaid shall determine at what intervals the circumstances, and in particular the nature of the investment, make it desirable to obtain such advice as aforesaid, and shall obtain and consider such advice accordingly.

(4) For the purposes of the two foregoing subsections, proper advice is the advice of a person who is reasonably believed by the trustee to be qualified by his ability in and practical experience of financial matters; and such advice may be given by a person notwithstanding that he gives it in the course of his employment as an officer or servant.

(5) A trustee shall not be treated as having complied with subsection (2)

 or (3) of this section unless the advice was given or has been subsequently confirmed in writing.

(6) Subsections (2) and (3) of this section shall not apply to one of two or more trustees where he is the person giving the advice required by this section to his co-trustee or co-trustees, and shall not apply where powers of a trustee are lawfully exercised by an officer or servant competent under subsection (4) of this section to give proper advice.

(7) Without prejudice to section eight of the Trustee Act, 1925, or section thirty of the Trusts (Scotland) Act, 1921 (which relate to valuation, and the proportion of the value to be lent, where a trustee lends on the security of property) the advice required by this section shall not include, in the case of a loan on the security of freehold or leasehold property in England and Wales or Northern Ireland or on heritable security in Scotland, advice on the suitability of the particular loan.

APPLICATION OF SS. 1–6 TO PERSONS, OTHER THAN TRUSTEES, HAVING TRUSTEE INVESTMENT POWERS

7.—(1) Where any persons, not being trustees, have a statutory power of making investments which is or includes power—

(a) to make the like investments as are authorised by section one of the Trustee Act, 1925, or section ten of the Trusts (Scotland) Act, 1921, or

(b) to make the like investments as trustees are for the time being by law authorised to make,

however the power is expressed, the foregoing provisions of this Act shall with the necessary modifications apply in relation to them as if they were trustees:

Provided that property belonging to a Consolidated Loans Fund or any other fund applicable wholly or partly for the redemption of debt shall not by virtue of the foregoing provisions of this Act be invested in any manner specified in paragraph 6 of Part II of the First Schedule to this Act or in wider-range investments.

(2) Where, in the exercise of powers conferred by any enactment, an authority to which paragraph 9 of Part II of the First Schedule to this Act applies uses money belonging to any fund for a purpose for which the authority has power to borrow, the foregoing provisions of this Act, as applied by the foregoing subsection, shall apply as if there were comprised in the fund (in addition to the actual content thereof) property, being narrower-range investments, having a value equal to so much of the said money as for the time being has not been repaid to the fund, and

accordingly any repayment of such money to the fund shall not be treated for the said purposes as the accrual of property to the fund:

Provided that nothing in this subsection shall be taken to require compliance with any of the provisions of section six of this Act in relation to the exercise of such powers as aforesaid.

(3) In this section "Consolidated Loans Fund" means a fund established under section fifty-five of the Local Government Act, 1958, and includes a loans fund established under section two hundred and seventy-five of the Local Government (Scotland) Act, 1947, and "statutory power" means a power conferred by an enactment passed before the passing of this Act or by any instrument made under any such enactment.

APPLICATION OF SS.1–6 IN SPECIAL CASES

8.—(1) In relation to persons to whom this section applies—

(a) notwithstanding anything in subsection (3) of section one of this Act no provision of any enactment passed, or instrument having effect under an enactment and made, before the passing of this Act shall limit the powers conferred by the said section one;

(b) subsection (1) of the foregoing section shall apply where the power of making investments therein mentioned is or includes a power to make some only of the investments mentioned in paragraph (a) or (b) of that subsection.

(2) This section applies to—

(a) the persons for the time being authorised to invest funds of the Duchy of Lancaster;

(b) any persons specified in an order made by the Treasury by statutory instrument, being persons (whether trustees or not) whose power to make investments is conferred by or under any enactment contained in a local or private Act.

(3) An order of the Treasury made under the foregoing subsection may provide that the provisions of sections one to six of this Act (other than the provisions of subsection (3) of section one) shall, in their application to any persons specified therein, have effect subject to such exceptions and modifications as may be specified.

SUPPLEMENTARY PROVISIONS AS TO INVESTMENTS

9.—(1) In subsection (3) of section ten of the Trustee Act, 1925, before paragraph (c) (which enables trustees to concur in any scheme or arrangement for the amalgamation of a company in which they hold securities with another company, with power to accept securities in the second company) there shall be inserted the following paragraph:—

   "(*bb*) for the acquisition of the securities of the company, or of control thereof, by another company".

(2) It is hereby declared that the power to subscribe for securities conferred by subsection (4) of the said section ten includes power to retain them for any period for which the trustee has power to retain the holding in respect of which the right to subscribe for the securities was offered, but subject to any conditions subject to which the trustee has that power.

POWERS OF SCOTTISH TRUSTEES SUPPLEMENTARY TO POWERS OF INVESTMENT

10. Section four of the Trusts (Scotland) Act, 1921 (which empowers trustees in trusts the execution of which is governed by the law in force in Scotland to do certain acts, where such acts are not at variance with the terms or purposes of the trust) shall have effect as if, in subsection (1) thereof, after paragraph (*n*) there were added the following paragraphs:—

   "(*o*) to concur, in respect of any securities of a company (being securities comprised in the trust estate), in any scheme or arrangement—

   (i) for the reconstruction of the company,
   (ii) for the sale of all or any part of the property and undertaking of the company to another company,
   (iii) for the acquisition of the securities of the company, or of control thereof, by another company,
   (iv) for the amalgamation of the company with another company, or
   (v) for the release, modification, or variation of any rights, privileges or liabilities attached to the securities or any of them,

in like manner as if the trustees were entitled to such securities beneficially; to accept any securities of any denomination or description of the reconstructed or purchasing or new company in lieu of, or in exchange for, all or any of the first mentioned securities; and to retain any securities so accepted as aforesaid for any period for which the trustees could have properly retained the original securities;
   (*p*) to exercise, to such extent as the trustees think fit, any conditional or preferential right to subscribe for any securities in a company (being a right offered to them in respect of any holding in the company), to apply capital money of the trust estate in payment of the consideration, and to retain any such securities for which they have subscribed for any

period for which they have power to retain the holding in respect of which the right to subscribe for the securities was offered (but subject to any conditions subject to which they have that power); to renounce, to such extent as they think fit, any such right; or to assign, to such extent as they think fit and for the best consideration that can reasonably be obtained, the benefit of such right or the title thereto to any person, including any beneficiary under the trust".

LOCAL AUTHORITY INVESTMENT SCHEMES

11.—(1) Without prejudice to powers conferred by or under any other enactment, any authority to which this section applies may invest property held by the authority in accordance with a scheme submitted to the Treasury by any association of local authorities [or by the London County Council][6] and approved by the Treasury as enabling investments to be made collectively without in substance extending the scope of powers of investment.

(2) A scheme under this section may apply to a specified authority or to a specified class of authorities, may make different provisions as respects different authorities or different classes of authorities or as respects different descriptions of property or property held for different purposes, and may impose restrictions on the extent to which the power conferred by the foregoing subsection shall be exerciseable.

(3) In approving a scheme under this section, the Treasury may direct that the Prevention of Fraud (Investments) Act, 1958, or the Prevention of Fraud (Investments) Act (Northern Ireland), 1940, shall not apply to dealings undertaken or documents issued for the purposes of the scheme, or to such dealings or documents of such descriptions as may be specified in the direction.

(4) The authorities to which this section applies are—

(a) in England and Wales, the council of a county, a [county, metropolitan or other][6] borough (including a borough which has been included in a rural district), an urban or rural district or a parish, [a river authority][7], the Common Council of the City of London, [the Greater London Council][8] and the Council of the Isles of Scilly;

(b) in Scotland, a local authority within the meaning of the Local Government (Scotland) Act, 1947;

(c) in any part of Great Britain, a joint board or joint committee constituted to discharge or advise on the discharge of the functions of

Words in brackets repealed as from 1 April 1965 by the London Government Act, 1963.
Words in brackets inserted by Water Resources Act, 1963.
Words in brackets inserted as from 1 April 1965 by the London Government Act, 1963.

any two or more of the authorities mentioned in the foregoing paragraphs (including a joint committee established by a combination scheme under Part I of the Local Government Superannuation Act, 1937, or of the Local Government Superannuation (Scotland) Act, 1937;

(d) in Northern Ireland, the council of a county, a county or other borough, or an urban or rural district, and the Northern Ireland Local Government Officers' Superannuation Committee established under the Local Government (Superannuation) Act (Northern Ireland), 1950.

POWER TO CONFER ADDITIONAL POWERS OF INVESTMENT

12.—(1) Her Majesty may by order in Council extend the powers of investment conferred by section one of this Act by adding to Part I, Part II or Part III of the First Schedule to this Act any manner of investment specified in the Order.

(2) Any Order under this section shall be subject to annulment in pursuance of a resolution of either House of Parliament.

POWER TO MODIFY PROVISIONS AS TO DIVISION OF TRUST FUND

13.—(1) The Treasury may by order made by statutory instrument direct that, subject to subsection (3) of section four of this Act, any division of a trust fund made in pursuance of subsection (1) of section two of this Act during the continuance in force of the order shall be made so that the value of the wider-range part at the time of the division bears to the then value of the narrower-range part such proportion, greater than one but not greater than three to one, as may be prescribed by the order; and in this Act "the prescribed proportion" means the proportion for the time being prescribed under this section.

(2) A fund which has been divided in pursuance of subsection (1) of section two of this Act before the coming into operation of an order under the foregoing subsection may notwithstanding anything in that subsection be again divided (once only) in pursuance of the said subsection (1) during the continuance in force of the order.

(3) If an order is made under subsection (1) of this section, then as from the coming into operation of the order—

(a) paragraph (b) of subsection (3) of section two of this Act and sub-paragraph (b) of paragraph 3 of the Second Schedule thereto shall have effect with the substitution, for the words from "each" to the end, of the words "the wider-range part of the fund is increased by an amount which bears the prescribed proportion to the amount by which the value of the narrower-range part of the funds is increased";

(*b*) subsection (3) of section four of this Act shall have effect as if for the words "so as either" to "each other" there were substituted the words "so as to bear to each other either the prescribed proportion or".

(4) An order under this section may be revoked by a subsequent order thereunder prescribing a greater proportion.

(5) An order under this section shall not have effect unless approved by a resolution of each House of Parliament.

AMENDMENT OF S.27 OF TRUSTS (SCOTLAND) ACT, 1921

14. So much of section twenty-seven of the Trusts (Scotland) Act, 1921, as empowers the Court of Session to approve as investments for trust funds any stocks, funds or securities in addition to those in which trustees are by that Act authorised to invest trust funds shall cease to have effect.

SAVING FOR POWERS OF COURT

15. The enlargement of the investment powers of trustees by this Act shall not lessen any power of a court to confer wider powers of investment on trustees, or affect the extent to which any such power is to be exercised.

MINOR AND CONSEQUENTIAL AMENDMENTS AND REPEALS

16.—(1) The provisions of the Fourth Schedule to this Act (which contain minor amendments and amendments consequential on the foregoing provisions of this Act) shall have effect.

(2) The enactments mentioned in the Fifth Schedule to this Act are hereby repealed to the extent specified in the third column of that Schedule.

SHORT TITLE, EXTENT AND CONSTRUCTION

17.—(1) This Act may be cited as the Trustee Investments Act, 1961.

(2) Sections eleven and sixteen of this Act shall extend to Northern Ireland, but except as aforesaid and except so far as any other provisions of the Act apply by virtue of subsection (1) of section one of the Trustee Act (Northern Ireland), 1958, or any other enactment of the Parliament of Northern Ireland, to trusts the execution of which is governed by the law in force in Northern Ireland, this Act does not apply to such trusts.

(3) So much of section sixteen of this Act as relates to the Post Office

Savings Bank and to trustee savings banks shall extend to the Isle of Man and the Channel Islands.

(4) Except where the context otherwise requires, in this Act, in its application to trusts the execution of which is governed by the law in force in England and Wales, expressions have the same meaning as in the Trustee Act, 1925.

(5) Except where the context otherwise requires, in this Act, in its application to trusts the execution of which is governed by the law in force in Scotland, expressions have the same meaning as in the Trusts (Scotland) Act, 1921.

SCHEDULES

Section 1.   FIRST SCHEDULE

MANNER OF INVESTMENT

PART I

NARROWER-RANGE INVESTMENTS NOT REQUIRING ADVICE

1. In Defence Bonds, National Savings Certificates and Ulster Savings Certificates.[9]

2. In deposits in the Post Office Savings Bank, ordinary deposits in a trustee savings bank and deposits in a bank or department thereof certified under subsection (3) of section nine of the Finance Act, 1956.

PART II

NARROWER-RANGE INVESTMENTS REQUIRING ADVICE

1. In securities issued by Her Majesty's Government in the United Kingdom, the Government of Northern Ireland or the Government of the Isle of Man, not being securities falling within Part I of this Schedule and being fixed-interest securities registered in the United Kingdom or the Isle of Man, Treasury Bills or Tax Reserve Certificates.

2. In any securities the payment of interest on which is guaranteed by Her Majesty's Government in the United Kingdom or the Government of Northern Ireland.

3. In fixed-interest securities issued in the United Kingdom by any public authority or nationalised industry or undertaking in the United Kingdom.

[9] *See* Amendments by Statutory Instruments, *supra*, p. 68.

4. In fixed-interest securities issued in the United Kingdom by the government of any overseas territory within the Commonwealth or by any public or local authority within such a territory, being securities registered in the United Kingdom.

References in this paragraph to an overseas territory or to the government of such a territory shall be construed as if they occurred in the Overseas Service Act, 1958.

5. In fixed-interest securities issued in the United Kingdom by the International Bank for Reconstruction and Development, being securities registered in the United Kingdom.

6. In debentures issued in the United Kingdom by a company incorporated in the United Kingdom, being debentures registered in the United Kingdom.

7. In stock of the Bank of Ireland.[9]

8. In debentures issued by the Agricultural Mortgage Corporation Limited or the Scottish Agricultural Securities Corporation Limited.

9. In loans to any authority to which this paragraph applies charged on all or any of the revenues of the authority or on a fund into which all or any of those revenues are payable, in any fixed-interest securities issued in the United Kingdom by any such authority for the purpose of borrowing money so charged, and in deposits with any such authority by way of temporary loan made on the giving of a receipt for the loan by the treasurer or other similar officer of the authority and on the giving of an undertaking by the authority that, if requested to charge the loan as aforesaid, it will either comply with the request or repay the loan.

This paragraph applies to the following authorities, that is to say—

(a) any local authority in the United Kingdom;
(b) any authority all the members of which are appointed or elected by one or more local authorities in the United Kingdom;
(c) any authority the majority of the members of which are appointed or elected by one or more local authorities in the United Kingdom, being an authority which by virtue of any enactment has power to issue a precept to a local authority in England and Wales, or a requisition to a local authority in Scotland, or to the expenses of which, by virtue of any enactment, a local authority in the United Kingdom is or can be required to contribute;
(d) the Receiver for the Metropolitan Police District or a combined police authority (within the meaning of the Police Act, 1946);
(e) the Belfast City and District Water Commissioners;
(f) the Great Ouse Water Authority.[9]

---

[9] See Amendments by Statutory Instruments, *supra*, p. 68.

10. In debentures or in the guaranteed or preference stock of any incorporated company, being statutory water undertakers within the meaning of the Water Act, 1945, or any corresponding enactment in force in Northern Ireland, and having during each of the ten years immediately preceding the calendar year in which the investment was made paid a dividend of not less than five per cent on its ordinary shares.

11. In deposits by way of special investment in a trustee savings bank or in a department (not being a department certified under subsection (3) of section nine of the Finance Act, 1956) of a bank any other department of which is so certified.

12. In deposits in a building society designated under section one of the House Purchase and Housing Act, 1959.

13. In mortgages of freehold property in England and Wales or Northern Ireland and of leasehold property in those countries of which the unexpired term at the time of investment is not less than sixty years, and in loans on heritable security in Scotland.

14. In perpetual rent-charges charged on land in England and Wales or Northern Ireland and fee-farm rents (not being rent-charges) issuing out of such land, and in feu-duties or ground annuals in Scotland.

PART III

WIDER-RANGE INVESTMENTS

1. In any securities issued in the United Kingdom by a company incorporated in the United Kingdom, being securities registered in the United Kingdom and not being securities falling within Part II of this Schedule.

2. In shares in any building society designated under section one of the House Purchase and Housing Act, 1959.

3. In any units, or other shares of the investments subject to the trusts, of a unit trust scheme in the case of which there is in force at the time of investment an order of the Board of Trade under section seventeen of the Prevention of Fraud (Investments) Act, 1958, or of the Ministry of Commerce for Northern Ireland under section sixteen of the Prevention of Fraud (Investments) Act (Northern Ireland), 1940.

PART IV

SUPPLEMENTAL

1. The securities mentioned in Parts I to III of this Schedule do not include any securities where the holder can be required to accept repayment of the principal, or the payment of any interest, otherwise than in sterling.

2. The securities mentioned in paragraphs 1 to 8 of Part II, other than Treasury Bills or Tax Reserve Certificates, securities issued before the passing of this Act by the Government of the Isle of Man, securities falling within paragraph 4 of the said Part II issued before the passing of this Act or securities falling within paragraph 9 of that Part, and the securities mentioned in paragraph 1 of Part III of this Schedule, do not include—

(*a*) securities the price of which is not quoted on a recognised stock exchange within the meaning of the Prevention of Fraud (Investments) Act, 1958, or the Belfast stock exchange;

(*b*) shares or debenture stock not fully paid up (except shares or debenture stock which by the terms of issue are required to be fully paid up within nine months of the date of issue).

3. The securities mentioned in paragraph 6 of Part II and paragraph 1 of Part III of this Schedule do not include—

(*a*) shares or debentures of an incorporated company of which the total issued and paid up share capital is less than one million pounds;

(*b*) shares or debentures of an incorporated company which has not in each of the five years immediately preceding the calendar year in which the investment is made paid a dividend on all the shares issued by the company, excluding any shares issued after the dividend was declared and any shares which by their terms of issue did not rank for the dividend for that year.

For the purposes of sub-paragraph (*b*) of this paragraph a company formed—

(i) to take over the business of another company or other companies, or

(ii) to acquire the securities of, or control of, another company or other companies,

or for either of those purposes and for other purposes shall be deemed to have paid a dividend as mentioned in that sub-paragraph in any year in which such a dividend has been paid by the other company or all the other companies, as the case may be.

4. In this Schedule, unless the context otherwise requires, the following expressions have the meanings hereby respectively assigned to them, that is to say—

"debenture" includes debenture stock and bonds, whether constituting a charge on assets or not, and loan stock or notes;

"enactment" includes an enactment of the Parliament of Northern Ireland;

"fixed-interest securities" means securities which under their terms of issue bear a fixed rate of interest;

"local authority" in relation to the United Kingdom, means any of the following authorities—

(a) in England and Wales, the council of a county, a [county, metropolitan or other][10] borough (including a borough which has been included in a rural district), an urban or rural district or a parish, the Common Council of the City of London, [The Greater London Council][11] and the Council of the Isles of Scilly;

(b) in Scotland, a local authority within the meaning of the Local Government (Scotland) Act, 1947;

(c) in Northern Ireland, the council of a county, a county or other borough, or an urban or rural district;

"ordinary deposits" and "special investment" have the same meanings respectively as in the Trustee Savings Banks Act, 1954;

"securities" includes shares, debentures, Treasury Bills and Tax Reserve Certificates;

"share" includes stock;

"Treasury Bills" includes Exchequer bills and other bills issued by Her Majesty's Government in the United Kingdom and Northern Ireland Treasury Bills.

5. It is hereby declared that in this Schedule "mortgage", in relation to freehold or leasehold property in Northern Ireland, includes a registered charge which, by virtue of subsection (4) of section forty of the Local Registration of Title (Ireland) Act, 1891, or any other enactment, operates as a mortgage by deed.

6. References in this Schedule to an incorporated company are references to a company incorporated by or under any enactment and include references to a body of persons established for the purpose of trading for profit and incorporated by Royal Charter.

7. The references in paragraph 12 of Part II and paragraph 2 of Part III of this Schedule to a building society designated under section one of the House Purchase and Housing Act, 1959, include references to a permanent society incorporated under the Building Societies Acts (Northern Ireland) 1874 to 1940 for the time being designated by the Registrar for Northern Ireland under subsection (2) of that section (which enables such a society

[10] Words in brackets repealed as from 1 April 1965 by the London Government Act, 1963.
[11] Words in brackets inserted as from 1 April 1965 by the London Government Act, 1963.

to be so designated for the purpose of trustees' powers of investment specified in paragraph (*a*) of subsection (1) of that section).

Section 3.   SECOND SCHEDULE

MODIFICATION OF S.2 IN RELATION TO PROPERTY
FALLING WITHIN S.3 (3)

1. In this Schedule "special-range property" means property falling within subsection (3) of section three of this Act.

2.—(1) Where a trust fund includes special-range property, subsection (1) of section two of this Act shall have effect as if references to the trust fund were references to so much thereof as does not consist of special-range property, and the special-range property shall be carried to a separate part of the fund.

(2) Any property which—

(*a*) being property belonging to the narrower-range or wider-range part of a trust fund, is converted into special-range property, or

(*b*) being special-range property, accrues to a trust fund after the division of the fund thereof in pursuance of subsection (1) of section two of this Act or of that subsection as modified by sub-paragraph (1) of this paragraph,

shall be carried to such a separate part of the fund as aforesaid; and subsections (2) and (3) of the said section two shall have effect subject to this sub-paragraph.

3. Where property carried to such a separate part as aforesaid is converted into property other than special-range property,—

(*a*) it shall be transferred to the narrower-range part of the fund or the wider-range part of the fund or apportioned between them, and

(*b*) any transfer of property from one of those parts to the other shall be made which is necessary to secure that the value of each of those parts of the fund is increased by the same amount.

Section 3.   THIRD SCHEDULE

PROVISIONS SUPPLEMENTARY TO S.3 (4)

1. Where in a case falling within subsection (4) of section three of this

Act, property belonging to the narrower-range part of a trust fund—

    (*a*) is invested otherwise than in a narrower-range investment, or

    (*b*) being so invested, is retained and not transferred or as soon as may be reinvested as mentioned in subsection (2) of section two of this Act,

then, so long as the property continues so invested and comprised in the narrower-range part of the fund, section one of this Act shall not authorise the making or retention of any wider-range investment.

2. Section four of the Trustee Act, 1925, or section thirty-three of the Trusts (Scotland) Act, 1921 (which relieve a trustee from liability for retaining an investment which has ceased to be authorised), shall not apply where an investment ceases to be authorised in consequence of the foregoing paragraph.

Section 16.   FOURTH SCHEDULE

Minor and Consequential Amendments

1.—(1) References in the Trustee Act, 1925, except in subsection (2) of section sixty-nine of that Act, to section one of that Act or to provisions which include that section shall be construed respectively as references to section one of this Act and as including references to section one of this Act.

(2) References in the Trusts (Scotland) Act, 1921, to section ten or eleven of that Act, or to provisions which include either of those sections, shall be construed respectively as references to section one of this Act and as including references to that section.

2.—(1) [In the Schedule to the Building Societies Act, 1939 (which specifies the classes of additional security which may be taken into account in determining the amount of advances to members), in paragraph 4 for the words from "stocks" to the end there shall be substituted the words "narrower-range investments (within the meaning of the Trustee Investments Act 1961) " and in paragraph 6 for the words from "stocks" to the end there shall be substituted the word "investments".][12]

(2) Nothing in this paragraph shall be taken to prejudice the power of the Chief Registrar under section fifteen of the Building Societies Act, 1960, to extend the classes of additional security specified in the said Schedule.

3. The following enactments and instruments, that is to say—

    (*a*) subsection (3) of section seventy-four of the Third Schedule to the

---

[12] Words in brackets repealed by the Building Societies Act, 1962, s.131, Sched. 10.

8

Water Act, 1945, and any order made under that Act applying the provisions of that subsection;

(b) any local and personal Act which, or any order or other instrument in the nature of any such Act which, modifies paragraph (l) of subsection (1) of section one of the Trustee Act, 1925,

shall have effect as if for any reference to the said paragraph (l) there were substituted a reference to paragraph 10 of Part II of the First Schedule to this Act.

4.—(1) In section one of the Trustee Savings Banks Act, 1954, in paragraph (a) of subsection (3), the reference to the acceptance of deposits of money for the benefit of the depositor shall include a reference to the acceptance of deposits of money by a trustee, and subsection (1) of section eight of the Post Office Savings Bank Act, 1954, and subsection (1) of section twenty of the Trustee Savings Banks Act, 1954 (which relate to the settlement of disputes), shall apply to any depositor being a body of trustees and to a person who is or claims to be the successor in the trusts of any depositor being a trustee as those subsections apply to an individual depositor and to a person who is or claims to be the personal representative of a depositor.

(2) Nothing in the foregoing sub-paragraph shall be taken to prejudice section twenty-two of the Trustee Savings Banks Act, 1954 (under which deposits may be accepted from a person acting as a trustee on behalf of the depositor, the account being in the joint names of the trustee and the depositor).

(3) Subsection (1) of section fourteen of the Post Office Savings Bank Act, 1954, and subsection (1) of section twenty-four of the Trustee Savings Banks Act, 1954 (which authorise the investment of certain charitable and provident funds in savings banks), shall cease to have effect so far as they relate to trustees.

5. For the purposes of the provisions of the Post Office Savings Bank Act, 1954, and the Trustee Savings Banks Act, 1954, limiting the amount which may be received by way of deposit or ordinary deposit or for special investment, or the provisions of the last-mentioned Act restricting the making of deposits in more than one trustee savings bank, a person who is a trustee shall be treated separately in his personal capacity and in his capacity as trustee, and in the latter capacity separately in respect of each separate trust fund.

6. For the reference in subsection (2) of section one of the House Purchase and Housing Act, 1959, to paragraph (a) of subsection (1) of that section there shall be substituted a reference to paragraph 12 of Part II and paragraph 2 of Part III of the First Schedule to this Act.

Section 16. FIFTH SCHEDULE

REPEALS

Session and Chapter	Short Title	Extent of Repeal
63 & 64 Vict. c. 62.	The Colonial Stock Act, 1900	Section two.
2 Edw. 7. c. 41	The Metropolis Water Act, 1902	In section seventeen, subsection (4).
11 & 12 Geo. 5. c. 58.	The Trusts (Scotland) Act, 1921.	Sections ten and eleven. In section twelve, subsections (3) and (4). In section twenty-seven, the words from "including such regulations" to the end of the section.
15 & 16 Geo. 5. c. 19.	The Trustee Act, 1925	Section one. In section two, the proviso to subsection (1). In section five, paragraph (*a*) of subsection (1) and subsections (4) to (6).
18 & 19 Geo. 5. c. 43.	The Agricultural Credits Act, 1928.	Section three.
19 & 20 Geo. 5. c. 13.	The Agricultural Credits (Scotland) Act, 1929.	Section three.
20 & 21 Geo. 5. c. 5.	The Colonial Development Act, 1929.	In section three, subsection (3).
24 & 25 Geo. 5. c. 47.	The Colonial Stock Act, 1934	The whole Act.
8 & 9 Geo. 6. c. 12.	The Northern Ireland (Miscellaneous Provisions) Act, 1945.	Sections four to six.
11 & 12 Geo. 6. c. 7.	The Ceylon Independence Act, 1947.	In the Second Schedule, paragraph 4.
12, 13 & 14 Geo. 6. c. 1.	The Colonial Stock Act, 1948	In section two, subsection (3).
2 & 3 Eliz. 2. c. 62.	The Post Office Savings Bank Act, 1954.	In section four, subsection (4).
5 & 6 Eliz. 2. c. 6.	The Ghana Independence Act, 1957.	In the Second Schedule, paragraph 4.
5 & 6 Eliz. 2. c. 60.	The Federation of Malaya Independence Act, 1957.	In the First Schedule, paragraph 8.
6 & 7 Eliz. 2. c. 47.	The Agricultural Marketing Act, 1958.	In section sixteen, in paragraph (*a*), the words from "or for the time" to "Act".
6 & 7 Eliz. 2. c. 55.	The Local Government Act, 1958.	Section fifty-four.
6 & 7 Eliz. 2. c. 64.	The Local Government and Miscellaneous Financial Provisions (Scotland) Act, 1958.	Section sixteen.

Session and Chapter	Short Title	Extent of Repeal
7 & 8 Eliz. 2. c. 33.	The House Purchase and Housing Act, 1959.	In section one, paragraph (a) of subsection (1), and subsection (5).
8 & 9 Eliz. 2. c. 52.	The Cyprus Act, 1960.	In the Schedule. in paragraph 9, sub-paragraphs (1), (3) and (4).
8 & 9 Eliz. 2. c. 55.	The Nigeria Independence Act, 1960.	In the Second Schedule, paragraph 4.
9 & 10 Eliz. 2. c. 16.	The Sierra Leone Independence Act, 1961.	In the Third Schedule, paragraph 5.

Index

Accounts
  beneficiaries' right to, 58
  duty of trustee in relation to, 44, 47
Accumulations
  rule against,
    under Law of Property Act, 1925, 65
    under Perpetuities and Accumulations Act, 1964, 65
Advancement
  presumption of—
    husband and wife, 22
    persons *in loco parentis*, 22
    rebuttal, 22
  statutory power of, 46
Agents
  power to appoint, 29
Alienation of property
  restriction on power, void, 14, 63
Allhusen *v.* Whittell, rule in, 41
Apportionment
  equitable
    Chesterfield's Trust rule, 41
    Howe *v.* Dartmouth rule, 38
  statutory
    appropriation of investments, in case of, 37
    not applied under rule in Howe *v.* Dartmouth, 41
Attorney-General
  action by, to enforce charitable trust, 16
Audit
  under Public Trustee Act, 1912, 44
  under Trustee Act, 1925, 44

Bailment
  distinguished from a trust, 3
Bank account
  should be in name of all trustees, 28
Bankruptcy
  settlements void in, 27
  settlements voidable in, 27
Bearer securities
  duty of trustee, 28